Hollywood,

Haunted Temples,

Demons

Presented are dozens of personal true accounts of how demons were cast out of people, a haunted house, and how people become walking haunted temples. Also, information reveals how evil spirits can have a connection with some Hollywood lifestyles.

Danny Frigulti

All Scripture is from the King James Version.

Acknowledgements
Special thanks to Chuck Romer for help with the cover design and Dave with editing. Most of all, thank you Lord Jesus for protection.

ISBN — 9781705966723

Other books available by the author on Amazon:

Are Yoga & Reiki Healing Evil?

Questions for Word-Faith Prosperity Believers

EXPOSED: The False Faith Healing-Prosperity Gospel

Are Word of Faith Televangelists Misleading Millions?

Biblical Counseling for people with Demonic Problems

Author's website is
www.dannyfrigulti.com

Historical Insight on Stonehenge

The cover picture of Stonehenge presents a controversial history. Some believe it is not a place of ceremonial offerings to gods or demonic spirits. Others believe Stonehenge is a religious site and has a direct connection with demon activity and gods. And some believe it was only a place for public gatherings. If it was erected for public gatherings, why all the work to set up what appears to be a circular pattern of huge stones that still cause people to wonder how ancient man was able to do this? And what occurred at the public gatherings? It is common knowledge that witches meet in groups in circles to invoke power from demonic spirits and worship them.

From what I have read, Archaeologists have not found any evidence that the people, who lived in Stonehenge over the centuries, were followers of the true God of the Bible. Old Testament Biblical history includes the timetable when Stonehenge was built. If this is a religious site, it was *not* set up to honor the Almighty God of creation, but to honor and worship other gods. You are entitled to your own belief.

Concerning the Contents of this Book

Dozens of examples about demonic cases cited in this book are also found in my book titled *Biblical Counseling for people with Demonic Problems,* which gives details on how to carefully discern evil spirits and counsel people. Providing understanding from different Greek words, it also explains how demons can invade a Christian's body. The repeated examples in this book are recorded for the purpose of emphasizing the violent, invisible spiritual realm and its impact on human lives. New cases, such as the first twelve, that begin the *Teachings from Various Demonic Cases* section, and some new cases about Tammi's ordeal, will have an * before them.

Table of Contents

To those who read this book:

Please do not take the information presented in this book in an entertaining manner. The suffering and pain I have seen demons do to people is happening around the world more than you realize. For some, it takes years for full recovery from the relentless wickedness of demons that cause extreme spiritual, emotional, and mental damage.

Acts 4:12 teaches that salvation comes from Jesus alone, and that we must be saved from our sins by no other name under Heaven. In this world, it is wise to stand before Jesus and receive Him as your Lord and Savior, with your sins forgiven. Because if you die in your unforgiven sins, and stand before Him at the Judgment, you will not ever enter Heaven, a place of holy worship.

Opening Comments

My purpose for writing this book is to alert people that there is a furious invisible war being waged by Satan and his legions of demons, and the impact of the war has become more visible. However, the first word in my book title reveals my main audience is Hollywood. But why Hollywood? The answer is simple. There is a tremendous amount of witchcraft being presented in movies, music, TV commercials, award specials, and the lifestyle of successful and popular people. New Age Mysticism, white witchcraft, and various forms of demonic activities are being practiced.

The influence of various Hollywood productions and music concerts have a phenomenal influence on viewers, which includes young children and teenagers. When one looks at the list of singers and actors that have overdosed on drugs or committed suicide, it is disheartening and shocking. Apparently, success, drugs, beauty, and money are not enough to give them peace and stability. God's guaranteed answer for peace is found in Jesus, the Prince of peace (Isaiah 9:6).

As a person who has listened to, counseled, and worked with dozens of men and women with demonic problems, I am convinced there is an invisible war that is influencing the increasing rate of these suicides and mishaps. The power behind these tragedies is the power of legions of invisible demons. This last statement may shock you, and you might have your doubts, but remain open-minded.

Please read the numerous cases in this book before you make your conclusion that evil spirits are not influencing the suicide and overdosing rate in Hollywood and around the world. I have had many encounters with demons, which gives me extensive knowledge on the deceptive powers of demons. Former witches have also helped me to understand the mind-controlling influence of demons.

When I had been a Christian for a few years, I prayed to Jesus to show me what first century Christianity was like. The content of this book will show you how He answered my prayer. I have seen four instant miraculous physical healings, have seen many demons cast out of people, and lives changed overnight.

Jesus has taught me to demonstrate with love, forgiveness, and discernment, not with public signs declaring the sins of others. No such behavior was found among the early Christians. These demonstrations misrepresent the Gospel message which encourages Christians to share the Gospel in a loving manner. Jesus taught Christians to love one another (John 13:34-35). Jesus also taught that His followers are to love those they believe are their enemies (Matthew 5:43-44; Luke 6:27, 35).

I don't look for demons. They look for me, because with Christ's love and authority, I wage war against them by helping people with demonic problems. My attitude and eyes are fixed on Jesus for His protection and guidance to those who need help (Colossians 3:1-2; Hebrews 12:2-4).

Some might call me an exorcist, but a minister of deliverance is more accurate. I've had to chuckle a few times when people have asked me if I charge money to cast out demons. I am not for hire. Freely, I received my calling and gift from God, so freely I help those in need. If I have to travel out of town, I ask people to cover my gas money. And if they want me to stay overnight, a couch or recliner is sufficient. I don't eat much food when involved with these situations.

One important requirement is always discussed in advance of any who seek my help from demonic problems. They must make a commitment to follow Jesus. And the people who sought help for them must realize the support needed *after* Jesus has set the person free. When demons are cast out, they build up an attitude of revenge. So long-term support is vital.

For the world, GPS means "Global Positioning System." This system moves people all over the world. For the Christian, GPS represents "God's Positioning System." His positioning system is found in prayer, the Bible, and moves us to our knees. It gives us the victory over everything.

I have chosen to not type out most of the Scriptures for the readers. There is a reason for this. Anyone who reads this book should look up and read the verses to have a better understanding of the ferocious and constant battle people face around the world. People have become lazy when it comes to reading and knowing the Bible. Don't be lazy. If you are, you will be deceived easily by the invisible supernatural power of the world that promotes evil and wickedness (2 Corinthians 4:3-4; 1 John 5:19).

Demons Are Vicious Soul Hunters

People of Hollywood: I have written this book with love to warn you about numerous spiritual dangers I have seen and confronted. Let me be your friend by alerting you to a powerful, deceptive, and vicious lifestyle that has current and eternal consequences.

Long ago, the LORD was speaking in dreams and visions when men were in a deep sleep upon their bed. During this sleep, He would open their ears and seal up their instruction (Job 33:14-16). As you will see in the next chapter, the dream He showed me was His will for me before I became a Christian.

1

An Unusual Dream at Age 6

I was born in 1946. At about six years old, I had a violent and unusual dream. Before I reveal the contents of it, I need to give you some background on my religious exposure as a child. Both sides of my family are Italian. My grandparents were immigrants from different parts of Italy. Thus, my religious upbringing was strict Roman Catholic. Hearing the Mass repeatedly in Latin did little for my Biblical growth. It did not lead me to Christ. I call myself a Christian, not a Catholic, because true Christians follow the Lord Jesus and His teachings only. The last sentence was not meant to bash on Catholics, but to alert them that they may not be born-again (John 3:3-8), and Jesus said this is *the way* to enter/see the kingdom of God.

As a young boy, I always heard the Mass in Latin so every Sunday was a repetition of the previous Sunday with a Rosary hanging in my hand. I did not read the Bible, and I was never told about the devil and demons prior to having this dream.

The dream was violent and frightening. I was screaming and yelling mean and angry words at an ugly creature in my dream. My voice was so loud that my loving mother was awakened. She ran from her bed to awaken me and asked me to explain my dream to her.

Here is my dream: I told her I was in a dirt field surrounded by a wall of fire, and I couldn't get out. In front of me was the devil, and he was taller than me. He kept saying he was going to get me and was trying to grab me. While screaming at the devil, I was trying to hit and scratch him. I was doing all I could to keep him from getting a grip on me when mom awakened me. It was a great relief to see my mother.

My mother was shocked to hear the content of my dream. She knew that I had never been told about the devil or demons. Therefore, she also knew that this dream was not a coincidence, and that evil would be pursuing me as I grew into a man. My precious mom, along with a neighbor named Irene, prayed for me for several years asking the LORD to watch over me. They both sensed an evil around me at times.

Their years of prayer were answered in January, 1974, when I truly repented of my sins and asked the Lord Jesus to come into my life as my Lord and Savior. My parents and friends could see Jesus at work in me within a few months. Jesus brought me closer to my family and has continually taught me the importance of loving people.

My mother now knew the dream I had when I was a child would become reality as I served the LORD. Within one year, I was being directly exposed to demon activity, as will be confirmed by detailed information that will be presented in various real life demonic encounters. My dream was an advance warning describing a portion of God's calling in my future life as a Christian for serving Jesus.

As a family, my parents and my sister also became true born-again believers in the Lord Jesus. The Holy Spirit brought to our attention some false teachings we had been taught in the Catholic Church we attended for decades as a family. We threw out rosaries, statues of Mary or any so-called saint, any type of idol, and no longer prayed to the Virgin Mary, because Jesus and the apostles never taught prayer to Mary.

I am not putting Catholics down, and I am not saying they are all dead in their sins. However, they *must not* depend on the Pope or a priest to forgive (absolve) their sins. Jesus takes away our sins (John 1:29). He is God's only Savior (John 3:16-17; Acts 4:12), and His shed blood from His *one-time sacrifice* (Hebrews 7:27; 10:14) cleanses us from all our sins.

Catholics must also realize that Jesus never taught about a place called Purgatory where a "partially forgiven" sinner can go for a "purging time" to have their sins completely forgiven. No one must depend on lit candles, backed by money, or another person's Rosary prayers or personal prayers to forgive their sins. Forgiveness of our sins comes *only* through the shed blood of Jesus (Matthew 26:28; 1 John 1:9-2:2). To say the shed blood of Jesus is not as good as lit candles, money, and Rosary prayers dishonors the blood and words of Jesus. No religious denomination can forgive the many sins we all commit.

Sincerely repent (turn away from them) of your sins according to Scripture, and Jesus will forgive your sins. Jesus is the only Savior the heavenly Father has given to the world for access to Heaven after death.

I had no idea what Jesus had in store for me when I became a Christian. As you read through the information provided and numerous demonic face-to-face encounters I've seen, my prayer is that you will not be preoccupied with demon activity. Rather, give Jesus first place in all things (Colossians 1:18), and stimulate each other to love, good deeds, and gathering in His Name (Hebrews 10:24-25). God bless you. Lead people to God's love and forgiveness through Jesus. Do this and I will look forward to seeing you in Heaven.

2 Corinthians. 4:17

For our light affliction, which is but for a moment, worketh for us a far more exceeding and eternal weight of glory.

2

Taken to a Horrible Place

I had been a Christian for about three years when an unusual event occurred in my life. One evening, while shopping at the Bible bookstore in Fresno, California, I felt different. After a few minutes, I wanted to go to my apartment and pray. Upon leaving the store, my mind was fixed on prayer and asking the LORD what was happening in my life. The feeling I had was unlike any I had experienced since I had become a Christian.

As I entered my apartment, I went to the living room and began praying on my knees. After several minutes, I realized that something was about to occur in the room. Gently I was taken out of my body and escorted straight down through my floor into the regions of the earth. Someone was holding on to my right arm, and it probably was an angel. I asked the person where we were going. He said, "Wait and you will see."

It was strange seeing various layers of rock. Eventually we came to an open area below the layers, and I was placed on an edge close to this pit of suffering. What I saw next was horrible. In front of me was a lake of darkness that had flames in it. Inside the lake were many people screaming in pain and rage. As they noticed me, some cried out for help, and others tried to reach for me and pull me in to suffer with them.

In my mind, I thought "Lord, why are you showing me this place. I know it exists because the Bible talks about it?" Suddenly I began to fall forward into this horrible place of suffering. I cried out to Jesus to help me. Just before I lost my balance, an invisible power of love grabbed me and stood me straight up. I said, "Lord, why did You almost let me fall into this place?" His response was "I am sending you to help people so that they will not end up in this place. Do not fall into their deception."

The last sentence is more in depth than it appears on the surface. Jesus had some specific evil areas for giving testimony about Him where I would be sent. This did not mean I would work only in these areas of powerful

21

deception, but that much of my life of telling the truth about the real Jesus to the unsaved would be confronting people who were entrenched with false belief and demon activity. The lake of darkness and flames was an indicator of how determined some are to ignore and reject Christ for the forgiveness of their sins.

Often I have tried to convince Mormons, Jehovah's Witnesses, New Age participants, and those involved with various forms of witchcraft, even Satanism, to repent and receive Jesus as their Lord and Savior. It isn't easy, because some are demon indwelled already or demon-controlled by demons around them. Yet, in order for me to have a proper spiritual relationship with Jesus, I must obey His calling to confront these people with an attitude of love for their eternal well-being.

Firmly I was taken up from this pit of suffering and put back into my body. Certain people I saw in agony and suffering stood out in my mind. The majority of people I saw in suffering down there were pretty women. Yet at times, their faces would change into an ugly appearance. All men know the "pretty power" a woman can convey to seduce a man for money and sex. The Book of Proverbs gives details about the sexual determination of women who are set on getting their way. Let's look at some of these Proverbs that describe seductive women.

Proverbs 2:16 – This is a warning to avoid strange/immoral women who seduce with flattering words.

Proverbs 5:3-8 - The lips of a strange/immoral woman are as honeycomb and smoother than oil, so remove your way far from her.

Proverbs 5:20-21 – Men are warned to not be enraptured with an immoral woman, and that the LORD sees all these things.

Proverbs 6:23-29 – This section of Scripture begins by telling men to know instruction is the way of life, to keep way from an evil woman who displays a flattering tongue, to not lust after her beauty, and to beware of her alluring eyelids. In verse 26, it describes such women as whorish, also known as a harlot. Verses 27-28 describe the spiritual anguish that awaits a man who indulges in this ungodly activity. And a final warning about indecent sexual activity (adultery) is recorded.

Proverbs 7:10-23 – An extensive list of Scriptures again details how an immoral/harlot woman acts like she is pure, but sets up her house in advance to participate in forbidden sexual activity (adultery) when her husband is gone.

Proverbs 23:27 – This verse describes a harlot/whore as a deep ditch and a narrow pit.

Proverbs is known as a book of wisdom. The wisdom presented from these numerous verses repeatedly warns people about the consequences of sexual immorality. Both men and women from Hollywood, and those who are in other areas of the world, are often involved with fornication and various types of sexual sin. However, Hollywood, with its films and TV shows, seems to glorify the forbidden sexual activities mentioned in Proverbs, the book of wisdom. Are you following God's wisdom?

One can only wonder where humanity gets its moral guidelines, if not from the Bible. Doing as your unbridled sex drive desires has led to divorces, sexual infections, deadly diseases, rapes, kidnaps, murders, physical assaults, incarcerations, and broken homes that cause extensive grief for children.

This horrible place of suffering I was taken to for observing those who persist in various forms of evil and *never* repent (ask the LORD to forgive their sins and follow Jesus) is real. Each person chooses *forever* to go "up to live" with the true God forever or "go to a place" where there is no comfort ever. Jesus is waiting for you to accept His forgiveness for all of your sins (John 1:12; 3:16-17).

23

Matthew 16:24

Then Jesus said unto His disciples, If any man will come after Me, let him deny himself, and take up his cross, and follow Me.

A Dream Teaches Me Demonic Discernment

I had been a Christian around 5-6 years when I had an amazingly clear dream about how to discern demon activity when it came upon people to influence them. This dream was not anything I was seeking in prayer. God gave it to me for helping in future areas where I would be around Christians who would verbally assault me and not realize a demon was using them for verbal evil.

It also showed me how to be cautious of men or women when these discernable facial and verbal attitudes emanated from people. This dream was prophetic, and if you don't agree with what I just said then follow *the future details* contained in this dream.

Another typical night, prayer before bed and then sleep greeted me. What happened next in a dream was astounding. This dream was so clear and sequential in all that I saw. I will present the details and how the dream became reality over the years in my life.

The dream began by showing me several men standing and one man kneeling to my right in front of the men. A man with a woman on each side of him was seated in front of the standing men. I could only see the face of the kneeling man, a man I had never seen, because he lived in Reno, Nevada, at the time of my dream. The veiling of the faces had a purpose. All the people with veiled faces in the dream would become my friends in the future. Jesus was veiling them from me to teach me how evil Christians, if they are Christians, can be when coming under demonic influence.

A voice of authority in the dream said three words: "Look. Listen. Learn." One by one, I watched these people come under demonic control from demons outside their bodies. The demons would come to their heads from behind and speak to their mind. The result was instant anger toward me. Exposing how each individual underwent a personality change with harsh language directed at me was a great teaching for discerning demon activity when it controls and influences people. Demons like to work through people close to us because our hurt intensifies.

Almost 40 years later, the three words in that dream still help me with discerning demon activity from unsaved people and Christians. The reason the faces were veiled was for me to not know in advance how my friends would hurt me and betray me. Each time one of the people in the dream hurt me deeply, I would remember the dream. Then I could see their face before me and see how the demon influenced the person. At different times over a 35 year span, these people made an effort to hurt me with no purpose except self-exaltation.

About two years ago, the face of the last person to my left in the dream was exposed to me. He was a friend of over 35 years, and his wife helped him hurt me deeply. I explained to both of them how they were under demonic oppression in their house and *exactly* how and what town the demons in their house came from. Both had active occult influence before becoming Christians, and have had struggles with demonic harassment.

Upon receiving my detailed letter, which explained their demonic oppression problem, they broke the friendship of over 35 years with a short note and chose to eliminate any chance for discussion. This supports the fact that they were under demonic deception. They have not talked to me since that time, but have made an effort to speak evil about me to people in different states.

This prophetic dream helped me to understand the unpredictable nature of man. It prepared me for hurt and suffering. And best of all, it moved me closer to my personal Lord and Savior, Jesus. Being hurt and deserted by close friends should not come as a surprise to those who read the Bible, because there is a record of a friend leaving the apostle Paul. In 2 Timothy 4:10, Paul says "Demas hath forsaken me, having loved this present world." Our best friend is Jesus. He will never leave us, forsake us, or deceive us (Hebrews 13:5).

When watching Christian television, I have seen men and women come under demonic influence when they preach falsely about Jesus.

An Evil Spirit of Many Names

In the Bible, the devil (Lucifer) is referred to by several names. These names and titles that describe his evil functions are recorded to reveal how Satan and his demonic spirits deceive mankind. Isaiah 14:12, 15 reads:

> How art thou fallen from heaven, O Lucifer, son of the morning! *how* art thou cut down to the ground, which didst weaken the nations! … Yet thou shall be brought down to hell, to the sides of the pit (KJV).

In this verse, a spiritual being named Lucifer is mentioned, yet most translations omit this name. Who is this important spirit? This is the one who was given this name *before* he was cast out of his heavenly residence because of his proud, arrogant, and insubordinate plans that are mentioned in verses 13-14. And his sinful life grows continually with the help of his legions of demons. When not permitted to dwell in heaven any longer, the Bible reveals that Lucifer is also called Satan, the devil, and many other names which describe his deceptive agenda against humanity.

On pages vii-viii in his book titled, *WHICH VERSION IS THE BIBLE?*, Floyd Nolen Jones details how the translators of different versions have chosen to disregard the obvious Hebrew (*helel, ben shachar*) in Isaiah 14:12. The proper translation of these words is "Lucifer, *son* of the morning," not "O *star* of the morning." Revelation 2:28 and 22:16 call the Lord Jesus "the star of the morning" or "the morning star."

There is a major difference between the phrase "the star of the morning" when compared to the phrase "son of the morning." Do not insult the Son of God by teaching the devil is the "morning star," because *only* Jesus, the Lord of Lords, is worthy of this brilliant description. Jesus is the true light. Satan is the false light.

Scripture identifies this evil one (Lucifer) as the devil, Satan, and other names that describe his functions which cause tremendous suffering upon humanity. As we learn more about "the evil one," it will be shown that he has legions of demons who are also relentless in afflicting people worldwide with oppression.

Though the name "Lucifer" is mentioned one time in the Bible, this does not mean he no longer is a spirit of interest or concern. He is described and identified by other names such as the serpent in Genesis 3. Revelation 12:9 and 20:2 expose him by multiple names as the devil, the great dragon, the old serpent, and Satan. In Job 1-2, he is again called Satan. Ephesians 2:2 calls him "the prince of the power of the air," and 1 Peter 5:8 labels him as "your adversary the devil." Thus, we see clearly from Genesis to Revelation, Lucifer is identified by many names and titles which denote his power and evil activity in the world.

Several references to demons from *The New Strong's Exhaustive Concordance* are listed to show how often they are found in Scripture:

1. The dragon is mentioned more than a dozen times in Revelation.
2. Satan, our adversary, is listed over 50 times in Scripture.
3. Devils, also translated demons, are found afflicting people over 100 times in the Bible.

These three points of information confirm we have many invisible enemies whose constant goal is to bring suffering into the world. It's hard to know how many demonic spirits are in the world. Referring to angels, Revelation 5:11 says "the number of them was ten thousand times ten thousand, and thousands of thousands." If you multiply this out, you come up with a huge number. I bring this up because Revelation 12:4 teaches that the dragon (Satan) "drew the third part of the stars of heaven and did cast them down to the earth." The stars represent angels (Job 38:7).

If a third of the angels rebelled, were cast out of Heaven, became demons and now follow Satan, we have a lot of evil upon the earth. Let's cling to Jesus, the Rock of our salvation and our deliverance!

5

Scriptures That Teach Demon Activity

From Genesis to Revelation, the Bible contains many verses and examples of demon activity in the world. When I became a Christian in 1974, many pastors in both conservative and charismatic churches were teaching their spiritual flock (1 Peter 5:1-4) about the reality of demon activity in the world. Christians were being taught about the armor of God in Ephesians 6:10-18. This section of Scripture is a reminder about what some call "The Invisible War," a war that visibly is deceiving multitudes.

Today, fewer pastors preach and educate their congregation on the importance of understanding our "invisible demonic enemy." The result is many Christians are under the oppressing power of demon activity, and this is evidenced by the lethargic attitude found in American Christianity. Counselors are spending many exhausting hours trying to find the main problem that continually brings people back into their office. Seldom are pastors and counselors taught how to discern demonic influence in Bible or seminary classes. Thus, the invisible problem that causes the visible problem cannot be discerned for helping those in need of total healing.

In the Garden of Eden, the serpent (also called the devil, Satan, and dragon in Revelation 20:2) was at work to deceive Adam and Eve (Genesis 3:1-7). God permitted him to be in a place of created perfection that God called "very good" (Genesis 1:31). No sin had ever occurred in this Paradise from God. Yet the LORD *allowed* the demonic serpent "to enter" the Garden. Keep this in mind when we later look at the various ways demons are found in churches and around Christians.

Satan's global deception to persuade and trick people to sin against the LORD has been ongoing throughout history. He has legions of demons that don't sleep, and they look for ways to make people suffer spiritually, emotionally, mentally, and physically. The various cases that will be presented later will confirm demons are vicious, wise, and they use our sins to gain access to oppress us in different ways. Demons hate Jesus and all people, so don't be deceived into believing some demons are nice.

Our first Scripture teaching about demons among people was found in Genesis 3. Not every verse on demons will be covered. Let's continue our journey through parts of the Bible to expose numerous ways evil spirits that hate Jesus mingle with people and wreak havoc in their lives.

1 Samuel 15-16: When King Saul *disobeyed* the Lord's direct command to destroy all the Amalekites and their animals (1 Samuel 15), dire consequences came into his life. In verse 23, the prophet Samuel conveys the seriousness of King Saul's rebellion and says it "is as the sin of witchcraft."

Job 1-2: The Book of Job is a classic example of how Satan hates those who serve the LORD. His legions of demons have this same hate that has intensified over the thousands of years they have seen God bless people. When reading Job 1:7, it becomes quite clear that Satan is always looking for ways to oppress people on the earth (1 Peter 5:8).

After reading chapters 1-2, we find the devil's intent upon humanity is to bring as much suffering as the LORD will allow. Notice that God sets limits and guidelines. Day and night, demon activity focuses their attack worldwide on the followers of Christ (Revelation 12:10). However, the cleansing power of His blood and their testimony of faithfulness to Jesus bring the victory (verse 11). Verbal testimony about Christ's love and forgiveness, along with a constant fruit-bearing lifestyle (Galatians 5:22-23), glorifies God. Let's do it.

Old Covenant Demonic Sacrifices: Leviticus 17:7 says "they shall no more offer their sacrifices to devils, after whom they have gone a whoring." Deuteronomy 32:16-18 reveals the Israelites had turned away from and forgotten the God Who formed them. They provoked the LORD to jealousy with sacrifices to devils. Psalm 106:35-39 details the explicit sins of mingling among the heathen, learning their sinful ways of life such as serving idols, sacrificing their sons and daughters to idols, and shedding innocent blood which defiled them.

These evil decisions are shocking! So why did God's people do such horrible things? Upon reading Jeremiah 44:15-19, we find that when these people chose a demonic lifestyle, they served demons and were rewarded in various ways for their satanic worship. From demons, they received food and protection (verse 17). Evil spirits enjoy counterfeiting the blessings of God, because it gives them control over the participants.

Demonic Events Found in the Gospels

The Gospels record numerous times that Jesus encountered evil spirits and how He displayed His authority over them. Before He went out in ministry to fulfill Isaiah 61:1-3, He was led into the wilderness (Matthew 4:1-2) for a 40 day fast to prepare for the most victorious ministry in our history. Matthew, Mark, and Luke teach us about the demonic encounters Jesus faced and give important insight to us.

Matthew's Gospel: 4:1-11, 24; 8:16, 28-34; 9:32-34; 10:8; 12:22-30; 13:19; 15:21-28; 16:21-23; 17:14-21.

Mark's Gospel: 1:21-27, 29-34; 3:11, 22-30; 4:15; 5:1-17; 7:24-30; 9:17-29.

Luke's Gospel: 4:1-13, 33-36, 40-41; 6:17-19; 8:26-29; 11:14-26; 13:10-16; 22:31-32,

These Epistles Confirm Demonic Interference

Acts 5:1-11, 16; 8:7; 16:16-18; 2 Corinthians 2:10-11; 12:7-9; Ephesians 4:26-27; 6:10-18; Colossians 2:13-15; 1 Thessalonians 2:18; 1 Timothy 4:1-2; James 4:7; 1 Peter 5:8; Revelation 2:12-17.

The Revelation of Jesus Christ lays out the final vicious, worldwide battle between the LORD and Satan. O victory in Jesus, our Savior forever! Read the entire 22 chapters and get a blessing as stated in verse 3. Though not all Biblical examples of demon activity were listed, enough were cited for all to be well-educated on Satan's ways and works. Demons don't ignore us. Therefore, willful ignorance of spiritual warfare is disobedience to the LORD. We are responsible for wearing the armor Jesus has provided (Ephesians 6:10-19). Suit up and become an overcomer (1 John 4:4).

Old and New Testament verses presented in this chapter portray a definite demonic battle against followers of the LORD. God's inspired Word (2 Timothy 3:16-17) has been preserved for our protection so that we will have a loving and growing relationship with Jesus. The devil and his legions of demons don't sleep. Their primary intent is to keep people from seeking and finding Christ's forgiveness. And when one is forgiven, evil spirits continue to work at blocking God's love (1 Corinthians 13) and daily spiritual fruit-bearing (Galatians 5:22-23).

The following verses explain the demonic power that fights against Christ's Gospel of love and forgiveness. Many people don't realize that the demons in the air above us are worse than the particulate air pollution.

2 Corinthians 4:3-4

But if our gospel be hid, it is hid to them that are lost: In whom the god of this world hath blinded the minds of them which believe not, lest the light of the glorious gospel of Christ, who is the image of God, should shine into them.

Ephesians 6:11-12

Put on the whole armour of God, that ye may be able to stand against the wiles of the devil. For we wrestle not against flesh and blood, but against principalities, against powers, against the rulers of the darkness of this world, against spiritual wickedness in high places.

6

Ways Demons Can Enter People

This short chapter will provide detailed insight into ways evil spirits are able to remain in a person's presence or enter a person's body. This includes Christians. Demons need a sinful reason to enter a person. I have seen 5 areas of sin where evil spirits were given access to afflict people in different ways. When people seek deliverance from demonic control, it is wise to cover these areas in counseling before the intended prayer or deliverance begins.

Concerning demonic counseling, some people will argue that using the 5 areas to be listed for explaining how sin opens the door for evil spirits is wrong, because it is "a method" used to determine demonic invasion. They say Jesus and the apostles never used these 5 ways to drive out demons, and they are correct. However, only Jesus had the Holy Spirit without measure (John 3:34), and His apostles had apostolic Holy Spirit authority. Their "method" was unique Holy Spirit power.

I do not know of anyone who has the healing ministry and deliverance ministry the first century apostles had. There are some who boast that they have this power and authority. However, their false doctrine fruit, craving for money, and questionable miraculous works of signs and wonders proves otherwise.

By definition, a method is "a procedure or process for achieving an end" (The Meriam-Webster Dictionary, 2004, p. 452). If a "method" for helping someone, who is in sin, does not go against Scripture, then it is not a sin. All 5 areas of concern are to expose sin for repentance to glorify the LORD. Individually, they reveal sin and the need for repentance.

Can you imagine telling a person filled with various demons this: "Just ask Jesus into your heart and the demons will leave?" If this worked every time, I would use it as "the perfect method" of deliverance. Though some have used this way for presenting the Gospel as "their method" of driving out demons every time, it is *not* a method that always fixes all demonic problems. And, did Jesus always use this method?

The same opponents of these 5 ways to expose demonic entry because of "a method" usually have their "method(s)" of leading a person to Christ. They use John 1:12; 3:16, Acts 2:38-39, or Romans 10:9-10, 13 to get a person saved. Are these "methods" of salvation wrong? No. They are different ways to lead a person to salvation in Jesus.

Christian counselors pray for their patients and spend hours with them talking about their problems. Is this a sin, because "detailed and long-term" repetitive counseling sessions are not found in various epistle verses for counseling those in need?

Sometimes, when discussing these areas with the one seeking help, a demon will manifest which proves that an evil stronghold is being exposed by the Holy Spirit. Proceed with authority as led by the Holy Spirit. Five areas of sin for exposing demonic strongholds while counseling those with demonic oppression are:

1. Known sins.
2. Forgotten sins.
3. Various objects with an occult connection.
4. Curses, hexes, or spells from Witches.
5. Generational demons that occult families pass down.

These 5 areas, which provide openings for demonic spirits, will be explained to show how demons use these areas for attacking people and afflicting them. These areas are 5 basic starting points to go over when helping people with demonic problems. Spend time in prayer seeking the LORD'S guidance before starting to ask questions.

1) Known Sins

Confessing known sins can cover all 5 areas in some cases. When people come for help from demonic problems, they are seeking "deliverance" from evil influence and control. Cover the sins listed in Deuteronomy 18:9-11 and their struggles with certain sins found in Galatians 5:19-21. Keep in mind that King David committed adultery and had Uriah, the Hittite, murdered (2 Samuel 11-12). Yet no demon invaded David's body. On the other hand, I know of a man who went to Europe for sex and more than one demon was cast out of his body *after* he became a Christian.

Make sure they know astrology is a sin as clearly detailed in Isaiah 47:12-15 and Daniel 2:2, 27; 4:7; 5:7, 11, 15. Have them repent in each of these areas as needed. Be sure to find out if they are involved with false teachings such as New Age belief, false Word of Faith doctrines, Yoga, Numerology, any Eastern mystical religious teachings, Greek Mythology, occult studies, or putting secular Psychology and Philosophy (Colossians 2:8) on the same level as the Bible.

Make sure the person is a Christian. If not, explain the Gospel to them and lead them to Christ. If they are not willing to repent, the deliverance will be futile, because whatever is cast out will have an open demonic door to return with more "evil friends" (Matthew 12:43-45).

2) Forgotten Sins

During spiritual preparation for the deliverance session, pray that the Holy Spirit would reveal any sin that has been forgotten or is being demonically shielded from exposure. I have been in the middle of counseling sessions and the demonized person became aware of a forgotten sin, would confess the specific sin, and a demon would leave without even being commanded to leave the person.

Also, it is good to have people read selected verses out loud to see if this brings to remembrance any sins that should be confessed. Don't be shy to seek the help of the Holy Spirit. He is always ready to help those in need. He comforts (John 14:16), strengthens, empowers, and guides those in times of affliction. Sometimes, Christian friends who are called to help in the deliverance, can bring to remembrance a sinful choice that the demonized person has forgotten. Prayer always reveals answers.

3) Various Objects with an Occult Connection

Demonic objects such as statues of gods, incense/candle burning cups or holders, books, pictures of idols, good luck charms from any culture, letters from occult practitioners, clothing used in occult rituals, charmed jewelry, amulets, makeup used to gain demonic recognition, stones or crystals that are supposed to have occult energy coming out of them, talismans, dream catchers, Ouija boards, Tarot cards, or any good luck item that is connected to superstitious beliefs must be destroyed! They are not to be given away or put in a garage sale (Acts 19:18-20). Don't bring an abomination (a banned object) into your house (Deuteronomy 7:26).

Forbidden objects, those that have their origin in the occult and are used in the occult to activate demons, are contact points for evil spirits and bring curses because of our sins of disobedience. At times I have seen occult literature or demonic contact objects removed and thrown away, and demons have quickly left the person or their place of residence. It must be remembered that all occult objects do not automatically bring a demon into your house. However, the occult objects that have had a curse put on them will open the door for demons in your house.

Wealthy people, who have traveled the world, have a tendency to buy and collect various objects from different cultures. Some of these items have a direct link to the occult, because they were fashioned by people in witchcraft for the purpose of attracting evil spirits into the presence of the purchaser. Does your Hollywood home have any of these objects?

Evil spirits thrive on deception. Ignorance of Bible-forbidden objects gives them ongoing openings to develop a residence for inducing "spiritual bondage to deception." Demons will not overlook ignorance that is connected with their works of darkness. Even if unknowingly you receive or purchase an occult object, you jeopardize peace in your house.

Numerous times, when helping people get demons out of their house or out of their body, occult objects such as statues, good luck omens, books on New Age Mysticism, pictures of evil, and books about witchcraft have given demons a spiritual right to stay in the house or person. When these

Holy Spirit "banned objects" were removed and destroyed, the demons left and peace was restored to the people and their house.

Some people believe demons indwell physical objects. I don't go along with this view, because there is no Gospel account of Jesus casting demons out of physical occult objects of iron, stone, or wood. For a demon to stay in a physical object restricts its ability to deceive outside the object throughout the day. At times, the demon will stay *around* the object to draw the attention of people to view the object as a sacred relic. And the demon might follow a specific person during the day speaking words and thoughts of guidance. This is called "mind control."

When people gather around an object, that in any way represents the evil spirit realm, the demons can speak to their minds with words of deception or use what some call "thought transfer." As long as the forbidden/banned object is in the house, the demons will have spiritual grounds for entry to the residence. Those who collect Bible-banned objects have an urging and tendency to buy more of them. The enticement from demons to buy and display banned demonic objects that are displayed for all to see only increases the possibility of more demons in the house or building.

4) Curses, Hexes, or Spells from Witches

This section explains demonic curses, hexes, and spells sent from occult practitioners and witches. There is no such thing as a "good spell" for health or wealth. Any help from an evil spirit is always an evil curse. Though curses, hexes, and spells can be combined, their purpose varies. Later in case presentations of demonized people I have seen helped, I will cite instances where Christians "allowed" themselves to be put under the demonic influence of a curse or spell. Information from witchcraft sites will give us "their definitions" on these three ways they demonically afflict, counterfeit bless, and attempt to control people, even Christians. Later I will provide information where Christians had a spell put on them because of engaging in sin with a person who knew witchcraft.

World of Wicca — Witchcraft Curse

A curse is defined as "the invocation of **supernatural power** to inflict harm upon someone or something." To be able to put a curse on someone or something was considered a basic skill for a witch. Therefore, a curse is "An appeal or prayer for evil or misfortune to befall someone or something." (http://www.witchcraft.com.au/witchcraft-curse.html).

Witchcraft & Shamanism — Hexes & Curses
What is a Hex or a Curse?

The word "hex" originates from Pennsylvania Dutch. It was the equivalent of the German verb hexen, "to practice sorcery." ... By definition today, hex is an evil spell designed to cause harm to someone.... In today's world of Witchcraft, a hex is nothing more than a spell designed to carry negative manipulation to a person or a group of people.... A hex is like any other spell. It has a component for setting its intent, a statement of consequence and often the reason behind the hex. It includes calling upon some force or forces to help with the smiting and sometimes it can create a special method of delivery, such as through a demon, a talisman, or even a familiar (an animal who carries negative energy to the intended victim). (https://www.paganspath.com/magik/hex.htm).

Witchcraft Terms and Tools — Spells

Spells can be cast to affect the self, or directed to affect another person, and can be either beneficial or harmful. A positive spell is called a "blessing", although such archaic terms as "bewitchment" and "enchantment" are still sometimes used. Negative spells are generally known as "hexes" or "curses." ... A spell has a specific kind of formula, usually involving the use of incantations, images and implements (sometimes called "charms" or "runes") and a set of simultaneous actions, which are designed to gather magical power and direct it to a specific purpose. It can consist of a set of spoken or written words, a formula or verse, a ritual action, or any combination of these.... Spells may be cast by many methods, such as the inscription of runes or sigils on an object to give it magical powers, by the immolation or binding of a wax or clay image (poppet) of a person to affect him or her magically, by the recitation of incantations, by the performance of physical rituals, by the employment of magical herbs as amulets or potions, by gazing at mirrors, swords or specula (also known as scrying) for purposes of divination, and by other means. (http://www.witchcraftandwitches.com/terms_spell.html).

From what these three websites reveal about curses, hexes, and spells, it is obvious that people who use this occult power to activate "chosen effects" on people are invoking and using the supernatural power of evil spirits to accomplish their objective. And believing that only humans can put curses on people is not true. Demons can also perform occult rituals in the spirit realm. Constant prayer (Philippians 4:6; 1 Thessalonians 5:17) is the called lifestyle of any who help with deliverance from evil.

Without question, Hollywood has an abundance of psychics, New Age mystical beliefs, fortune-tellers, and those who promote various occult practices. Therefore, we should be open-minded to the fact that evil spirits operate and execute their influential ways upon numerous people in the Hollywood lifestyle. The invisible evil and manipulative power of curses, hexes, and spells display more control over people, contracts, and one's future than is realized.

A friend of mine, who became a Christian and is now with the Lord, was an accomplished witch for many years. She was educated on how to contact and conjure up evil spirits to carry out specific curses and spells. Knowing of my work in deliverance, she took time to explain the influence, effects, and control of curses and spells when directed toward certain people. When demons are given clear and direct instructions, they will use their time 24 hours a day, 7 days a week, to fulfill the required their goal.

Spells are often used to gain both physical and mental persuasion when interviewing for jobs. This occurs in Hollywood and in many areas of the world. Sensual spells can be used when interviewing for a job or specific role in a film. "Couch casting" interviews are well-known. Always pray that the Lord Jesus (Revelation 17:14) would annul and cancel *all* demonic interference with the interview.

5) Generational Demons That Families Pass Down

The topic of demons being passed down for generations in families often irritates people when discussing demon activity around Christians. Could ignorance on this subject be the problem, or could it be they have heard that demons can't be passed down through family generational lines? Don't put aside this question. Someone you know might need prayer.

It is common to find Christians who don't know anything about the sins or iniquities of the fathers being passed down to the children of the third and fourth generation. Also, there are those who are convinced that as soon as you become a Christian, no sins can be passed down through the family line. However, Numbers 14:18 says otherwise. Let's look carefully at what the Word of God has to teach us on this important topic.

Exodus 20:1-5 will provide our starting point to clear up confusion on this debated portion of Scripture. Verse 5 reads:

> Thou shalt not bow down thyself to them, nor serve them: for I the LORD God am a jealous God, visiting the iniquity of the fathers upon the children unto the third and fourth generation of them that hate Me.

God's warning is repeated in Deuteronomy 5:6-9. In these two areas of Scripture, the LORD is commanding His people not to bow down to any graven images (idols) and serve the demonic gods who support the worship of these idols of various materials. To do this would insult the LORD and give demons a higher place of recognition than the God of Israel Who brought them out of Egypt with great signs and wonders. The fathers are responsible for leading the family to the LORD.

What would be the iniquity and sin that the LORD would visit (pass down) to the children of the third and fourth generation? In this case, it would be demon activity, because bowing down to idols and serving them is direct worship to Satan and his demons. This is a consequence of *all* people, not just God's people, who become demon worshippers and do not repent prior to death. Anyone who seeks to make contact with evil spirits will open the door for demons in their presence.

In my exposures in helping people come to Christ, the ones with generations of family witchcraft always had demons around them or inside them. To break the clinging power of demonic bondage, a strong, "verbal renunciation" of what had been visited upon them was needed. They called upon the LORD and trusted in His power of forgiveness to annul all occult evil that had been passed down to them.

Also, they expressed forgiveness for those who had sinned against them by transferring demons into their presence without their permission. When open recognition of using demons for assistance is used, the demons will stay in the family line to build up power over generations according to Exodus 20:4-5. The evil transference of power must be rejected and renounced.

In his excellent book *Christian Counseling And Occultism*, Kurt Koch expands on the importance of understanding the "clinging generational power of demons" when ministering deliverance. Through decades of worldwide ministry experience to the oppressed, he says "Mediumistic gifts can be inherited, transferred, or acquired through dabbling with the occult."[1] To emphasize the needed awareness of occult generational transference to the Christian, Dr. Koch says:

> However, my own experience, which stretches back now for over 40 years, I have found that in as many as 50% of cases mediumistic gifts survive conversion. This is a source of great danger to a person's Christian life. If one subsequently discovers, therefore, that one is in possession of mediumistic powers, one is duty bound to ask God to remove them and to replace them with the gifts of the Holy Spirit.[2]

41

Dr. Koch's decades of personal involvement and accurate insight with hundreds of demonically oppressed individuals should not be ignored. Generational bondage can be passed on. In my years of reading literature from those with deliverance experience, Dr. Koch ranks at the top. Please remember, upon conversion, demons don't always "automatically" leave a family line that has been involved with generations of demon worship.

As an example, if demonic healing gifts were active in the family line, then these "passed down gifts of healing" can counterfeit the healing gifts of the Holy Spirit which *are not* passed down in families. The true gifts of healing are given *only* by the Holy Spirit as stated in 1 Corinthians 12:11. And all Christians do not have gifts of healing (verse 30). Other occult gifts, such as various forms of fortune-telling, mind-reading of active thoughts, and false prophecy, can also be passed down for generations.

There is an area of Scripture many use to teach that, upon receiving Jesus as Lord, all demon activity is removed from within and around the new Christian. We will take a close look at this position to see if the verses clearly teach: "As soon as you become a Christian, all demon activity is driven out of your presence and no generational witchcraft power can be passed on to you." Ezekiel 18:1-4 is the Scripture used to teach the LORD does not pass any of the father's sins down to his children. The verses read:

> ¹The word of the LORD came unto me again, saying, ²What mean ye, that ye use this proverb concerning the land of Israel saying, The fathers have eaten sour grapes, and the children's teeth are set on edge? ³As I live saith the LORD God, ye shall not have occasion any more to use this proverb in Israel. ⁴Behold, all souls are mine; as the soul of the father, so also the soul of the son is mine: the soul that sinneth, it shall die.

In these verses, there is no reference to eliminating the third and fourth generational visitation of the iniquities upon the children. So what is the LORD saying through the prophet Ezekiel? As you read down through the chapter, it becomes clear that the LORD is specifically talking about the sins committed by individuals that eventually lead to physical death. Living in spiritual death (not repenting of your iniquities, sins) follows you to your physical death. The entire soul dies.

Verse 5 presents a conditional statement when it uses the word "if." This means that "if a man be just, and do that which is lawful and right" according to verses 6-9, he shall live. The sons will not be punished for the sins of their fathers "if" they follow the LORD. The context of Ezekiel 18 contrasts the difference of walking in righteousness or living in sin. If a man continues doing evil, he shall die in his iniquity (verse 18). The soul that sins shall die (verse 20).

When understood, Ezekiel 18 teaches that when living a righteous life of repentance, the power of sin is broken and not passed down to the children. Yet, children have free choice. Pray for them daily, because this world is increasing in deception and wickedness. And "if" a father remains in his iniquities, the sinful effects of occult involvement can be passed down to his children. Drug and alcohol addicts also seem to place their children at a greater risk for these sinful addictions to be passed on.

We have covered and explained 5 basic ways demons enter the lives of people. The next section will explain dozens of demonic encounters I have witnessed. You will see verification for one or more of these 5 ways demons entered people. I will share what I did right and disclose mistakes I made so that you will not make the mistakes I made. Yes, I confessed all my mistakes as sin. I am clean before the Lord Jesus. Should you be called to minister to the demonically oppressed, prepare for a life of more prayer and fasting in specific situations (Matthew 17:21).

In the numerous cases of demon harassment that will be outlined in the next chapter, some will be Christians. Many believe it is impossible for a demon to indwell the body of a Christian. There is no teaching in the Bible that says a demon cannot be inside a Christian's body.

To use the common arguments that a demon cannot be inside the body of a Christian such as: 1) "Darkness and light cannot be in the same place,"

2) "You are sealed by the Holy Spirit," and 3) "You ae the temple of the Holy Spirit" do not teach immunity to demonic invasion for the Christian. And if a demon is inside the body, it does not affect the person's salvation.

My book *Biblical Counseling for people with Demonic Problems* devotes an entire chapter to explaining how demons can be in a Christian.

Endnotes:

1. Kurt E. Koch, *Christian Counseling And Occultism* (Grand Rapids, Michigan: Kregel Resources, 1994), p. 16.
2. Ibid., p. 17.

Note: Please consider getting the books I mentioned in these last two chapters by Kurt Koch and Merrill Unger if you are convinced the Lord Jesus wants you to help people with demonic problems. Or you might want to read them to better understand "demon activity among the saints."

Understanding Christ's Authority and Power

When using the Name of Jesus to cast out demons, it represents the authority and power found in His Name. It is His authority and power, not ours. We just can't use His Name *anytime* to overpower the enemy. Deliverance from demonic oppression manifests when we wait (God's timing) upon the Lord Jesus and are moved by the Holy Spirit to speak the Name of Jesus. Paul waited for Christ's perfect timing in Acts 16:16-18, and *then commanded* the demon "in the Name of Jesus to come out of her."

If the demonized person seeking help is not a Christian, share the Gospel to see if they are sincere about following Jesus. Sometimes, at conversion to Christ, the demon activity is removed by God's grace and no deliverance is needed. If they are resisting a commitment to serving Jesus, do you think He will give you His authority to cast out *all the demons* and leave the person spiritually empty and defenseless?

Remember to inquire if the person had any involvement with séances Astrology, fortune-telling, Numerology, Ouija board, Reiki healing, palm or Aura reading, or sought any information from the spiritual realm.

7

Personal Information About the Author

I was born on September 14th, 1946, and my parents always cared for me. Dad passed away in 1993, and my mother went to join him in Heaven in 2003. During the six months that followed their deaths, something unusual happened in my life. I had been told that these six months were usually a time of emotional difficulty and grieving. For me it was different. Though I missed being with them, something pre-planned happened in my life. During this time, the Lord Jesus was very gracious to me, because for months all I could remember about them was the way they loved me.

Constantly healing memories came to my thoughts, memories of the many ways they cared for me. I always had food, clothes, a bed, and the needed discipline. They took time to talk with me and encouraged me to give my best effort in whatever I did. A few days before I entered Kindergarten, my mom had a life-impacting conversation with me. This is what I remember her telling me:

1. You will be gone most of the day. When you come home, you will still obey us. Mom knew of the influence other kids could have on me.
2. Try your best in the classroom and outside at recess time when you are playing games.
3. You will be meeting kids you have never played with before. Show respect for everyone.
4. She paused for a few seconds and then said these words I have never forgotten: "Whether you believe it or not, God sees and knows everything."

Go back over these guidelines I was given, and you will know what kind of a mother the LORD gave me. She had amazing grace qualities. Dad also supported these guidelines. All of these words of wisdom helped shape my life to serve Jesus and treat people properly. As I looked again at the last sentence, I became choked with emotion and praised God for my parents. The world would be a better place if more people followed these guidelines. Because of our personal faith in Jesus as our Savior Who shed His blood and died for our sins, I know I will see them in Heaven forever.

My mother was a talented athlete. In high school, she set the school record for triple jump, a record that stood for many years. Her speed was exceptional. The track coaches wanted to train her for the Olympics, but her father said she was needed on the farm after school.

She was left-handed and taught herself how to pitch on her 60 acre farm. She put a target on the back of the barn and hit it with power and accuracy. Eventually she played semi-pro softball for about ten years.

Her pitching improved. At a softball tournament in San Luis Obispo, California, she struck out 17 of the 21 batters she faced. To top off her performance, she got the only hit of the game, a single. She stole her way around the bases and stole home for the 1-0 victory.

However, she accomplished another great achievement. In a game, she hit two grand slam homeruns in the same inning. She was the cleanup batter, and she knew how to clean up the bases when runners were on.

She made the best chocolate cake. It was so delicious that my friends wanted to know when cake was in the house. Here is what made her cake unique. She put as much frosting between the two layers as she put on the top of the cake. This made it saturated with flavor. And, she always made extra frosting so I could put it on graham crackers. Mmmn; so delicious!

My father was a produce manager for 29 years. We always had fruit and veggies in the house. He was quiet, but very observant concerning whatever happened in the house. He truly had a gift of discernment. More than once, he told me to be careful about a new friend I brought home. He was right on when it came to figuring out people. Every August, he told his wife to go shopping and get the two kids what they needed for school.

Here's the story of how, on a Sunday afternoon, he saved my life. I was scheduled to clean carpets in the San Jose area that evening. My trip would take me over Pacheco Pass, which is a winding road at times with gusting winds that sway your vehicle. Dad was sitting in his chair relaxing when suddenly he got up and went out to look at the front tires on my van. He motioned for me to come out of the house.

I went out to see what he wanted. He told me to look on the inside of the passenger tire. As I stooped down to see the tire, I saw a large bubble had bulged out on it. A new tire was put on for my trip. If my dad had not noticed the faulty tire, most likely a blowout would have occurred at 70 mph, and I would not be typing this information. My dad had discernment about people and dangerous situations. He also brought me joy by teaching me how to stream fish, hunt, and do yardwork.

My sister also became a Christian in 1974, about three months after my conversion. She has remained faithful to Jesus since that time. Growing up, she behaved mom and dad better than I did. She met a wonderful man of God after high school, and they have been married over 50 years.

As a little boy, I would rest on our backyard lawn during the summer nights and look at the many stars and wonder how God made so many. I also wondered how there could not be a wall to stop the stars or if they went on forever. I was captivated by God's creation, not knowing at that time all creation declares the glory of God (Psalm 19:1).

Growing was a blast! Sports participation was a part of my life. I was blessed with a body that could excel in different sports. I played quarter back when our sixth grade flag football team won the city championship. The city recreation department put together an all-city team of the best grammar school football players to play us — Jefferson elementary school.

The game was played on a cold Saturday morning at Recreation Park. We led the whole game and won 39-32. But there was more athletic fun to follow during this school year.

The city hosted a two-man basketball tournament for elementary school students. Left-handed Greg King was my partner. Games were played to 25. In the finals, it was 23-23 and I passed the ball to Greg. He drove across the free throw line and threw up a looping left-handed hook shot. Nothing but net! We were city champs. Greg scored 19 of our 25 points.

It was spring time and track was available, so I looked at different events and decided to focus on the long jump. I broke the city record by nearly a foot. Like my mom, I was physically gifted to excel in sports, if I made a strong effort.

Baseball was so natural for me. I tried out for Little League baseball when I was 8 years old. At that time, only three 8 year olds in Visalia had ever been drafted into the majors, and I became the fourth. I was stuck at second base my first season. In our final game, I turned a double play in the last inning to save our team from finishing in last place. My mom was ecstatic and gave me a dollar. This was back in 1954, when candy bars were a dime. I was so happy, because I could buy ten candy bars and share them with my friends.

Before I finished five years in Little League baseball, I had played every position except catcher and first base. During my final season, a former Pittsburgh Pirates third baseman was sitting by my mother at one of my games. This is what he told her: "Your son has more talent than any player in the league." Yet, I quit baseball during the last half of my fifth season, when I was second in the league in homeruns. This hurt my mother because of her success in softball. However, she never scolded me for my decision.

My first job was picking fruit in the fields when I was only fourteen. My pay was $1.10 an hour. It was the summer of my freshman year, and I wanted a car for my junior year. The hot weather and fuzz from the peaches made me want to quit at times, but I had a goal. My goal was to purchase a 2 door hard top 57 Chevy. For two more years, I worked at washing dishes after school and tossing pizzas. One day mom took me car shopping and I found my 57 Chevy. Finally, all the work paid off. Oh, I was happy! Time to roll down the windows and cruise.

Cruising Main Street in Visalia was a weekend attraction. It was just like Happy Days in our town – remember Arthur Fonzarelli, "the Fonz," and Ritchie Cunningham? We had car hops at different dining places in Visalia. We would meet at these places to eat, talk, play our radios, flirt with the car hops, and then go back to cruising the main drag. At the famous Merle's drive-in, we would gather for their generous offerings of French fries and large scoops of ice cream, while listening to the juke-box play our favorite songs.

Gas was 30 cents a gallon, so it was common for us to be cruising after midnight and listening to music. Our town was peaceful, and we had established friendships with the policemen. The Winchell's Donut shop on Mooney Boulevard was a stop for the policemen after midnight. We would go in and eat with them and drink hot chocolate. Because of their night shift, they drank coffee. Times have changed. Proper respect is not given to law enforcement officers who do their jobs properly.

While working at a pizza place, I became friends with the main cook. He mentioned he was going to sell his motorcycle. I bought his 1961 Triumph Bonneville. I rode it to the mountains, the beach, and one time to the Ventura area. The frame and cases were chromed. It had a tear drop gas tank, riser bars, and was painted candy apple red.

High school would begin a series of injuries that would occur every year I played football and continue until my junior year of college football, which was my last. I was successful as a placekicker and had scholarships offered to me after my sophomore year in junior college, but didn't want to go to any of the schools that offered me a scholarship.

In my sophomore year, I began to spend time with guys who did drugs. After months of watching them, I made the decision to try different drugs. Within a year, I was arrested for a $70 drug sale, and was sentenced to a year in the county jail. This crushed my parents and relatives. I began to consider suicide, because I had shamed my family name.

Many of my friends got into drugs. I watched some become heroin addicts, one a speed freak, some altered their brains with constant use of LSD, or combined alcohol with their drugs. I never became an addict. My use was occasional, and I stayed away from needles. One friend had a drug-linked seizure and choked to death on his own vomit while napping on his couch. Another left his wife and two children and chose heroin again. These past experiences now help me to understand and have compassion for the enormous drug problems in the music arena and Hollywood.

When I was released from jail, I began to work out harder than ever for football and prepared for the next season. I was now faster, stronger, and quicker. I set my eyes on a program that had a history of success.

My junior year was at the University of Alabama where I played for the legendary Paul "Bear Bryant" as a walk on. I remember asking God to let me have one season without an injury to see how well I could play football. I knew I was not good enough to play pro football, but so desired one injury free season to enjoy the game.

A torn groin muscle that bled past my knee kept me out for three weeks as a kicker but it didn't matter, because Richard was a better place kicker than me. When it healed, I was going to start on the kickoff team against Tennessee, our fourth game on the schedule. I was blessed with a quick start and could hit, so specialty teams and punt rush were where I could play. One day in practice, we had ten yard sprints. Only three players on the team were quicker.

On Thursday before the Saturday game in Birmingham, Alabama, I pulled a hamstring in my kicking leg and could not run. It took three weeks to heal, but my two injuries had taken their toll on me mentally. I turned in all my practice gear before the team flew for a Saturday night game in Baton Rouge, Louisiana, against those tough LSU Tigers.

Depression was intense in my mind constantly for failing to play one down for 'Bama.' My goal had been to get my name in the sports section so people would remember me for sports, rather than my previous drug problem. Also, I wanted to clean up my family name.

And then it happened. I had struggled with depression since I was a teenager. I was furious at God for not answering my prayer for only one injury free season of football. Never playing a down during a 'Bama' game convinced me I was a big failure. I looked around in Tuscaloosa and purchased 24 capsules that I thought were for sleeping. I was determined to take my life. To my surprise, I had made a deal for 24 speed capsules.

Within a few minutes after gulping these down, my high heart rate told me I had not bought sleeping pills. I went out and found a deal for 50 sleeping pills. I cursed God from my bed during this time, just waiting to die. Suddenly my heart rate became slow and irregular, and the beats were not happening much. My thought was, "Well I will be dead in a few minutes and have no problems."

As my heart stopped, I watched my soul come out of my body, and it was hurled into a place of darkness. Suddenly I was in front of a pool of still, dark water. It was a lonely place. I was all alone A rock was thrown from behind me and when it hit the water, it begin sinking. Immediately I saw myself as that rock drowning in darkness forever.

I was terrified, and began to call out to God to not let me drown in darkness forever (Jesus talked about outer darkness in Matthew 25:30). I did not ask Him to forgive my sins at this time, but continued to ask for His help. An invisible force grabbed me and quickly took me back to my dormitory bed in Tuscaloosa and stuck me in my body.

My friends knew I had been struggling with depression at this time and decided to drop by and see me. They looked at me on my bed and knew they had to take me to the hospital. They loaded me in a car and took me to the hospital. I felt like part of me was dead.

The doctor gave me fluids to make me vomit. Only empty capsules came up, and I passed out. My night was spent in the hospital, where my heart stopped at times. I remember nothing of that night.

Sometime during the next day, I woke up to a doctor looking at me. We talked about what had happened and how many drugs I had taken. She said I had taken enough drugs to kill two people and couldn't explain why I was alive.

Years later, when I became a Christian, I had the answer for what the doctor couldn't explain. Jesus kept me alive for the purpose of sharing His love and forgiveness to people around the world and for writing this book to help people in Hollywood and the music industry. The sharing would come through personal testimony to people of how Jesus changed my life for the better in various ways, through the books I would write, and sometimes traveling hundreds of miles to help demonized people.

I finished my education at Fresno State University, and became a Christian in January, 1974. Immediately I began sharing the Gospel of Jesus Christ. One day, while visiting my father, I asked him to forgive me for all the wrong things I had done that hurt him. He forgave me that day, and from that time we always had a relationship pleasing to Jesus.

A few years after I became a Christian, I was sitting in the Fresno State Student Union with my girlfriend in the afternoon. There weren't many people around. We were talking about Christianity and a young man walked up to our table. He asked to sit with us. For a few minutes, he listened to our conversation and then asked, "Is it true that Christians should be willing to die for their faith?" I said "Yes," and he pulled a handgun out of his coat. He pointed it at me and said, "Who's first, you or her?" I said "Me." He laughed, put the gun in his coat and left. We never saw him again on the campus. Was this to prepare me for the unpredictable fears that are part of a deliverance ministry that was soon to come?

Up to age 37, I had never met a lovely lady I wanted to marry, but that would soon change. In October, 1983, I visited a small church at a Sunday night service, and a lady caught my attention. She was tall, pretty, athletic, intelligent, blond, and her green eyes were captivating. We knew each other for nine months and were married. She knew of my work in helping demonized people and was willing to be alongside to assist me.

About a year after we were married, we had a discussion concerning my future employment. We decided that I should go back to college and pursue a teaching credential in Physical Education. It was the perfect decision. For over 25 years, I taught Physical Education, Health Science, coached volleyball, basketball, and softball. In 2014, I retired. When I "cruise" or walk, it is wonderful to see former students at different places in my hometown. So many wonderful memories!

During the births of our children, I was at her side. She never said a bad word in all the pain or blamed anyone for what she was enduring. It hurt me to see her in pain, and so after our last child was born, I told her: "Please, no more children." She agreed.

Concerning childbirth, there is something very important I want to address. Most women develop stretch marks from the expansion of raising the child in their womb during pregnancy. These marks should be viewed as marks of love that stretch out to embrace a child who is loved. The husband can put his cheek gently on the proper abdomen area to kiss and caress these marks to display love for his wife and love for the child. And if agreed, the husband can gently rub soothing lotions on "the love marks."

After 30 years, our marriage ended in divorce. I will always love her with more than a friendly love, but will not be "in love with her" as I once was. Thirty years is a long time to live with someone, love that person in many ways, and realize the marriage is finished. Jesus has provided the healing for my heart. I have given this divorce information, because some people like to probe for a fabricated tabloid story to make money.

Before the marriage was finished, I began preparing for the ministries and book writing God had put in my heart. I am 73 years old at this time (2019). Since the filing for divorce (2010), I have not personally held a woman's hand, hugged a woman passionately, or kissed a woman.

If I am to be married again at my current age of 73 or older, the LORD will have to send me an amazing lady. She must be faithful to Jesus and me, share the joy found in Jesus, stand when persecuted for her faith, be pretty, communicate well, and be willing to go through the oppression I encounter when helping demonized people. If there is such a woman, I will cherish her with God's love from above in many ways.

For the last 14 years, I have had several violent dreams where demons are watching me or attacking me. In one dream that was very violent, my son got up to awaken me. By my bed, it was cold. The next day my son told me the hallway walls were like ice, and when he entered his room, his room was ice cold. When these occur, I know that Jesus is letting me know that demons are aware of my current work, so I pray more, listen to music that edifies me, and meet with friends.

At times, I still struggle with depression. When it comes upon me, I know it's from evil spirits and resist it (James 4:7). And for comfort, I sleep with my Bible on my heart to fulfill Psalm 119:11 and John 17:17.

My days are spent in prayer, marveling at God's creation, preparing more books, working out at the gym, listening to praise music, telling people about the Lord Jesus, walking gently in my house with my hands lifted in praise to honor and worship the LORD, singing praises to His Name (YouTube offers a beautiful song called *I sing praises to His Name* by various musicians), thanking my Lord Jesus for His love and all the good memories, His corrections, and fellowshipping with friends from the two churches I attend (Colossians 3:16-17; Hebrews 10:24-25).

Sometimes, when listening to music, it feels like the music is being played inside me. Jesus has given me many blessings. My children, friends, fellow believers in Christ, flowers, birds, butterflies, mountains, meadows, streams, seashores, animals, and little children bring blessings to my eyes, ears, and heart. Children are adorable! All believers in Christ's love and forgiveness are God's little children (1 John 2:1, 12, 13, 18, 28; 3:7, 18).

There is more information I would like to reveal about this author who loves the Lord Jesus. I am all Italian. My grandparents came from different parts of Italy, and some of my uncles and aunts were born in Italy. Since I was little, my favorite food has not been pasta but ice cream. If ice cream were all protein, I would be all muscle. However at my age, I must limit my ice cream intake or I will go from "buff to puff." Seriously, I praise the LORD for ice cream and all His delicious and nutritious food.

When it comes to music, I like Gospel praise, traditional hymns, Maranatha Praise albums, some of the contemporary Christian music, music from the 50s – 70s, Country music, and instrumentals. The LORD has given humanity so many options in music to offer praise to the Name of Jesus. What turns me off in music is when the instruments are so loud you can't hear the words. Also, I don't care for a dissonance beat (a disruptive beat that brings in discord). The violin is my favorite instrument, and then I like the saxophone.

Two of my favorite instrumentals are *Theme from a Summer Place* by Percy Faith and *The Homecoming* by Hagood Hardy. When I hear the violins in these songs, I wish I could be a note on the strings being played and launched with love into the world, then coming back for more launches of love. This paragraph and the next should give you a look at my heart.

My innermost being is a combination of fine china and thin crystal, so I am easily hurt. Harsh words can crack my spiritual china and see-through crystal. So why did Jesus send a delicate person into a violent demonic world? The LORD does as He pleases (Psalm 115:3; Daniel 4:35). He would show me how Satan has crushed many, and I was to be a messenger of hope and help them by bearing their burdens and partaking of their deep hurts (Galatians 6:2).

Christians are ambassadors for Christ and are given the ministry of reconciliation (2 Corinthians 5:18-20). This is what true Christians do daily. We are gifted differently, because there are numerous needs among the many people of the world. The biggest needs are Christ's love and forgiveness. In my designated spiritual arena, I would describe myself as a little boy in a man's body who constantly needs Jesus' help: "Jesus please help me. You know that I am fragile."

Over the years, I have had demons appear in my house to harass me in a variety of ways to interfere with the ministry Jesus chose for me. One night when I was not home, my son and his date came by our house. My son wanted to change his shirt. His date stayed in the kitchen as he went to his bedroom. The lovely lady thought she heard me typing in the family room, so she went in to talk with me. As she looked into the room, she saw that I was not typing, yet the keyboard was being used by an invisible force.

She left the room and when my son came out of his room, she told him what she had seen. He went to the room and saw the same thing. A demon was using my keyboard. A few seconds after my son entered the room, the typing stopped. He told me about what happened.

The next day I opened up my Word documents to continue working on my first book. I found that paragraph indents had been changed and certain sentences and information had been put in areas of the book where they didn't belong. I spent hours carefully going through over 200 pages to make corrections. This taught me to pray each time I do the Lord's work on my computer.

Around 1980, I asked Jesus for a ministry of "love, wisdom, and truth." He has given it to me at a high cost. In recent months more tears have come out of me than at any time in my life. I feel so weak and uncomfortable when shaking as I cry, but I have learned that broken hearts get their healing from Jesus (Luke 4:18). Men have forgotten how to cry or just don't want to. Tears bond a marriage and glorify Jesus (John 11:35).

Due to job injuries and surgeries, I have pain daily. I don't like to take painkillers, so I have learned that my best way to control the pain is through obedience to Jesus and helping others. This strengthens me spiritually, mentally, and actually reduces my pain. And I go to the gym regularly.

Men, start making Teddy Bear hugs common. They are so much fun, as both of you try to find the best hugging and snuggling positions. "With words of love, make love often to your wife's heart." Demons hate love displayed in any way, because God is love (1 John 4:7-8). And love has more of an impact when you say "I love you" rather than "love you."

My children are 25-32 years old. Something I still do is hug the pictures of my children against my heart, pray for them, and thank God for them. Hopefully, the information that I revealed about me will move you to occasionally pray for me. Love from Above to you and your household forever. Below I will share something precious that came to me in my quiet time with Jesus.

Husbands, practice this wisdom:

For daily abundant life, treat your wife as your wedding day bride.

8

Defining Haunted Temples

When using the word "haunted," most people think of a place with evil spirits in it or around it that cause fear or a disquieting effect. This view is acceptable. But what about the definition of the word "temple"? Could it have another definition other than a building? Let's proceed to find the answer.

A basic definition of a temple is a building reserved for religious practice or a place devoted to a special or exalted purpose. Depending on what type of worship occurs in a temple, there can be demons that have been conjured through rituals to dwell inside. Contacts with evil spirits in temples is not uncommon. The usual religious reason for having spirits in a temple is to worship them for the benefits they can provide.

The word "temple" is recorded over a hundred times in the Bible in reference to a place of worship. Yet in some verses, it is used to describe the human body. With this in mind, let's learn what the Bible teaches about living human temples and find out if they can be haunted. I will list verses that clearly show people are also called temples, and we will see the purpose of living temples.

In John 2:19-21, Jesus refers to His body as "this temple" when He foretells His resurrection. Paul records in 1 Corinthians 3:16 that Christians "are the temple of God and the Spirit of God dwelleth" in them, and in verse 17 he says "for the temple of God is holy." Again Paul reminds the followers of Jesus in 2 Corinthians 6:16 that they "are the temple of the living God."

These verses establish that people are living temples. They are not stuck in one place like a constructed temple. But are all people *holy* living temples? The answer is "No," because not all people are indwelt with the Holy Spirit. Only those who have received Christ (John 1:12) and repented of their sins are indwelt with the Holy Spirit (Romans 8:9).

From the Bible, we learn that all people are living temples that move, but not all are temples of the Holy Spirit. The only ones who are temples of the Holy Spirit are those who have confessed they have sinned and then asked God to forgive their sins through the shed blood of Jesus (Matthew 26:28; Ephesians 1:7; 1 Corinthians 15:1-4). When this confession occurs, the Holy Spirit comes into the person (Ephesians 1:13), and their spirit is no longer dead in its sins.

The person who does not repent of their sins does not have God's forgiveness, and their spirit remains dead in their body. Though they are moving temples, they are moving temples of spiritual death. This means they will not be allowed into Heaven where people of eternal life dwell.

Since unforgiven people do not have the Holy Spirit in them, they don't have the Holy Spirit power from God to fight off demons. Therefore, people not indwelt with the Holy Spirit, including those in the music industry and Hollywood, are susceptible to constant demonic influence and control (Ephesians 2:2).

There are billions of human temples around the world. But how many are void of God's Holy Spirit? It is God's will for His Holy Spirit to dwell in as many people who will receive His forgiveness through His Son, Jesus Christ (Acts 2:38). No one is forced to repent of their sins and receive Jesus as their Lord and Savior.

Look back at the first sentence in this chapter where the definition of "haunted" was presented. Because of demons, it is clear that humans can be "haunted temples of fear and a disquieting effect." Jesus is the cure.

In the next section, numerous examples of demonic assaults on people will be listed. These examples will confirm that human temples can become "haunted demonic temples" when attacked by demons. However, there is "another way" humans can be haunted within. That way is the indwelling power of unforgiven sin, which can taunt and haunt. The cure and spiritual healing for this is committing your life to Jesus (Luke 4:18). It's your choice.

Teachings from Various Demonic Cases

As we move on to learn about numerous encounters I have had with demonically controlled people, I will explain how the LORD used me and friends to help them. My purpose for detailed explanation will be to educate the reader on how to discern demon activity around or inside people, and Biblical ways to set people free from demonic power. Each situation will be presented as a case. Instructions with details to freedom will accompany each example.

The demonic cases are not listed chronologically. Some of what I cite will be strange or amazing, but none of the works of demons is falsified or exaggerated. Those with experience in casting out demons know that from case to case, there is no consistent pattern of predicable behaviors. The schemes and wiles of the devil's spiritual world of demonic assaults upon humans have been operating for thousands of years. Various encounters presented will verify this.

Before numerous cases are cited, it is imperative to tell you that those who have ministered to demoniacs know that oppression and depression can come *upon* them and their helpers at different times. During the time of confrontation, the Holy Spirit empowers and protects the LORD's servants. Often for me, within a day after some deliverances, I would be tired and need rest in a quiet place for a day. And oppressive demonic retaliation is common among the demoniac's family. Pray constantly (Philippians 4:6).

Another fact to share is that some demoniacs go unconscious or semi-conscious during the deliverance, while others are aware of all that occurs. Also, sometimes when a demon is cast out, it happens within a few seconds. Other times I have seen it take over an hour to make one demon leave, as the demon rages, resists, and screams violently.

When discussing casting out demons, understanding what a Spiritist does must be explained. A Spiritist is one who *plans* and believes in "conjuring up or contacting" what they believe is the spirit of a departed person or another spirit for the purpose of gaining guidance in lifestyle, knowledge, or any self-desire. The Spiritist does not see the spirit it talks to as an enemy and will consult and converse with the spirit often.

The Bible clearly forbids us to be "a consulter with familiar spirits" (Deuteronomy 18:11) or have any contact with them *for witchcraft purpose* (Leviticus 19:31; 20:6). Some Christians use these verses to teach you should *never* ask a demon anything, even in a commanding tone.

The Bible confirms whether you should ever command or ask a demon *for any* information to proceed in a deliverance. Our answer is found in Mark 5:9. Jesus is speaking to a demon and says, "What is thy name? And he answered saying, My name is Legion: for we are many."

When Jesus asked the demon for his name, he was not consulting the demon to engage in Spiritism witchcraft. There was a purpose, but Mark does not specifically tell us why. I've seen cases where a minister never commanded a demon to give any information in a deliverance (just prayer and commands to "Leave in Jesus' Name"), and I've seen ministers who *carefully* limited any commands for information such as, "What sin allows you to be in this person?" Both were successful.

A careful reading of all the Gospel accounts where Jesus cast out evil spirits verifies they left quickly. Jesus was given the Holy Spirit "without measure" (John 3:34). Therefore, when He spoke His word to a demon, it was gone quickly. No one has ever had this type of success when casting out demons, not even His disciples (Matthew 17:14-21). The apostles were given authority to cast out demons, but still had to wait for the LORD's timing (Acts 16:16-19). Any who help demoniacs must pray and fast.

Let's take a look at numerous demonic cases and learn how to help people with demonic problems.

*Case 1: Demons in a Fraternity

My carpet and tile cleaning contract with a record store found me in San Diego for two weeks every four months. Knowing there were fraternities open for lodging because of summer school, I enquired about spending my nights at one of the houses. Their charge for spending five nights was reasonable, so I unloaded my suitcase. What I would encounter would jolt me and also give me the chance to present the Gospel to students.

There were several college students staying in rooms of the house, both boys and girls. Within a day, I began talking to people about Jesus and some of the demonic cases I had seen. Several were receptive, and the crowd of listeners grew. I was introduced to a Jewish student (Raphael), and he was aroused with interest in the details. We spent time together, and I also made it a point to share verses that showed Jesus was Israel's promised Messiah. Though he showed interest in the Scriptures I presented, he did not make a commitment to receive Jesus as his Messiah.

As the word spread about my work with demonized people, a person with a strange personality was introduced to me through my Jewish friend. One evening Raphael came to me and said that I should talk to the guy with the strange attitude, so we found him in his room. I introduced myself and began to talk about Jesus, His love, and forgiveness. Within a few minutes, the room became uncomfortable.

Suddenly his face began to change in appearance, and he was nervous as I talked to him about Jesus. His eyes would not look at my eyes, and his irises were turning dark. From previous demonic cases, I realized a person with indwelling demon activity was before me. For Raphael's protection, I decided to put my hand over his head and prayed for Jesus to protect him from the demons.

What happened next was amazing. The demonic person began shaking out of control and said, "I see a white light over Raphael's head!" I knew it was time to cast out the demon and commanded it to come out of him. One came out of his chest and went through the wall. Then a very ugly demon, shaped like a huge bat with large wings, came out of his head. The "bat demon" was small, then expanded to a wingspan of three feet as it disappeared through the ceiling. We all saw the demons. A peaceful presence was now evident.

As the spiritual climate settled in the room, I tried to persuade this young man to receive Jesus as his Lord and Savior, to have his sins forgiven, and to have Holy Spirit protection from demonic retaliation. He refused. This person had seen God's covering light over Raphael to protect him and had seen the demons cast out of himself in the Name of Jesus. Yet he would not even thank Jesus for removing the evil spirits.

The next day two girls came up to me and told me, that while in their room, they had felt the evil presence pass through their room. They wanted to know how to be protected from this evil. I explained the Gospel of God's forgiveness through Jesus, and they became Christians.

Teaching: Sometimes people have demons cast out of them and don't even thank Jesus. Pray that such people would surrender their heart to Jesus. The girls were wise. When they felt the awful presence of demons pass through their room, they wanted protection from this forever and found it in Jesus. Raphael was miraculously protected by Messiah Jesus' covering of light, and saw demons cast out of a person "in the Name of Jesus" However, he also refused to accept Jesus of Nazareth as His personal Messiah Who gave Himself as a sacrifice for the sins of the world (John 1:29; 3:16-17; 1 John 2:2).

*Case 2: A Demon Erupts in an Ice Cream Parlor

You already know that ice cream is my favorite food. It tastes good any time of the day or night. I was in Corte Madera, California, for a carpet cleaning job. For lunch, I wanted ice cream. When I found an ice cream place, I ordered a hot fudge sundae. The lady who served me had an accent, so I asked her about it. She said she was from Germany.

As I began to eat my ice cream, I prayed silently for God to open a door of conversation about Jesus. I was the only customer, so I asked her about religion in Germany and if many people went to church. Her response was a harsh "No!" I waited a few minutes and I asked her what she thought about Jesus. Instantly her voice took on a *masculine tone*, and she yelled these words at me; "I told you not to talk about religion!"

Because of my many experiences with demonic people, I realized a demon had spoken through her mouth. This was not the time to tell her about Christ and His forgiveness. I apologized to her for upsetting her and left the shop. The ice cream was still tasty.

Teaching: At this time, I had been a Christian for almost 10 years and had shared the Gospel of Jesus more than a hundred times. With two strong rejections to my questions and many multiple experiences with demonized people, I knew this was not the time to say any more about Jesus. Demons hate Jesus and the mention of His Name. Possibly this woman had previous occult involvement, because the demon raged out of her mouth at me for mentioning the Name of Jesus. I never went back to that business for ice cream again, but prayed that she would find Christ's love and forgiveness before she passed away.

*Case 3: Love Prevails at Dinner

San Jose was one of my contract obligations for carpet and tile cleaning. Every four months I stayed at Ginny's apartment and slept on the floor or the couch. She was a wonderful high school friend. When I revealed my work with demonized people, she showed an interest in learning the details. She also showed shaking, uneasiness, and did not make consistent eye contact during our conversations.

Ginny had a background in drinking, drug use, and immorality. With my understanding of ways demons enter people, I began to carefully observe her during our time together. She was open-minded to the fact that she might have demon activity in her life. I took this situation carefully, because I did not want to assume she was indwelled with a demon, try to cast it out, and find out I was wrong in my discernment. There was no reason to rush into this situation, because I knew I would see her every four months. I spent more time in prayer and conversation with her.

The four months went by, and again I was at her residence for a week of business. She had begun to spend more time in activating her Christian faith. One evening, before I went to clean carpets, we went to dinner. The conversation focused on Jesus. All of a sudden she let out a gasp and said: "It just left me. I don't feel any pressure in my head." I don't know whether this demon was inside her or attached to her head from the outside. Her face looked so relaxed, and she was happy! Her love for Jesus had created an atmosphere of love the demon could not bear to be around.

Teaching: Patience was needed in this case. During the months of time I did not see her, I was in prayer for her that Jesus would watch over her and that she would be set free. We didn't debate if the demon was inside or outside of her. We praised the Lord that it was gone.

*Case 4: Riding With a Demonic Driver

A friend had invited a college student to our Bible study. We spent time together and, as I began to observe his eyes and face during conversations, I wondered if he was indwelt with demons. He showed an interest in talking about demons in the world, so I asked him about his family and their background. His mother's side had witchcraft involvement. This was a situation where the demonic person was being coached from the inside on how to respond to my questions. I needed patience.

One day he picked me up and drove me to his house. Suddenly, he began to speed through traffic in a very unsafe manner. I told him to slow down, but it got worse. It was like sitting in a wild race car. He looked at me with a sneer and dark eyes that were not his normal eyes. It was clear that a demon was using him to drive the car in a reckless way.

I prayed silently and did not rebuke the demon. Slowly, Stanley came into full control of the car and slowed to normal speed. We arrived safely at his house. Though the demonic sneer had been visible on his face while driving, he was now back to a normal appearance.

Teaching: If you know a person is indwelt with demons, do not let them drive you anywhere. I could have driven to his house, which was ten minutes away, but he offered to come get me, and the demon had a plan for an accident. This was a time when I did not use good judgment, not realizing it was a demonic setup.

*Case 5: A Disagreement Ruins a Deliverance

A woman from Woodlake, California, called me, and asked if I would come to her house and help her husband who had demonic problems. I knew the couple and that her husband had demonic symptoms, so I told her I was on my way to pray for him.

When I arrived, they both greeted me. The man knew he had demons in him so we went right to work to cast them out. Spiritual things were going well and then the phone rang. It was a new friend of mine. I told him I was busy casting demons out of Dave. Bob replied, "But Dave is a Christian. There can't be demons inside him." I began to explain to Bob, from the Scriptures, how it was possible for a demon to indwell a Christian. He would not accept anything I said. Frustrated in my effort, I ended the call and quickly learned a valuable lesson. The Holy Spirit anointing I had when I began helping Dave was gone.

Suddenly it sounded like tree branches were cracking and breaking in the fields. Their horses began to run around wildly in the pasture. After a few minutes of prayer and rebuking the demons that were agitating the horses, peace came upon the horses.

His wife and I agreed that Bob had been led by a demon to call during the deliverance, and the demon knew that we were 50 miles from where Bob placed his call.

Teaching: Never allow a phone call to interfere with casting out demons. Don't argue doctrinal differences during a deliverance session. Pray that God would not permit the demons or disagreeing people to interfere with the deliverance. I never talked to Bob again about demons in Christians.

*Case 6: Occult Books Near My Head

My trip to Goleta, California, to meet Russ and his wife was pleasant. He wanted to buy a specific chemical from me for his tile cleaning in all-night stores and discuss any new insights I had on carpet cleaning. We enjoyed dinner and catching up on what was happening in our lives. I spent the night on the floor in his extra bedroom and an unexpected surprise was waiting for me.

Sleep did not come, so I prayed and my attention was directed to a book shelf about 3 feet from my pillow. I browsed through the spine titles and two books captured my attention. Both were occult books. One was *The Book of Shadows,* and the other was *The Book of the Dead.* Both of these are high-powered occult books for demonic contact. They are used for spells, curses, and various works of evil. I began to cast out all demon activity connected to these books. In a few minutes, I was able to sleep.

The next morning Russ told me, that from his room, he heard what I did. He said that demons passed through his bedroom wall and out. I explained the demonic teachings contained in the books, yet he would not renounce his occult involvement and receive Christ's forgiveness. I continued business with him but never visited his house again.

Teaching: When staying at a person's house, it is always important to pray for discernment and Christ's protection. Evil books can be in any room. Also, it is important to be aware of any statues of idols or paintings that portray supernatural evil.

*Case 7: The Doctor Wanted Help for His Son

A Christian lady was talking to me and encouraged me to meet with her friend who was a Chiropractor. She was concerned about his participation in witchcraft, specifically aura reading, which he used to diagnose pain areas in his patients. I went to his office and talked to him about the aura reading. He was convinced it was not evil in any way, so I left his office. This meeting laid a foundation to help his son.

Within a month, I received a call from the doctor. His son, Jake, and a friend had been conjuring up evil spirits in an occult ritual. Something went wrong in their ritual. The demons did not stay in their assigned area of the room. The demons began trying to invade their bodies. Jake resisted with all his strength. His friend didn't, and Jake told me he watched as a demon entered his friend.

The doctor asked if Jake could come to me for prayer. I met with Jake and he renounced his sin of setting up a ritual to contact demons. He was not indwelt with a demon, but had strong oppression around him, which caused him to shake as he confessed his sin. He shook during my prayer, as I commanded the demons to leave his presence. Jake gave up his occult involvement. However, his friend never came to me for help.

Teaching: Occult rituals do not always go as planned. The demons have more control during the ritual than most people realize. Since the doctor did not to give up his witchcraft practices, I never went back to have fellowship with him. Jake's experience taught him a valuable lesson. Curiosity can lure you into the occult.

*Case 8: Things Heat up in the Snow

One of my accounts was located in Tehachapi, California, a beautiful mountain community of about 10,000 when I visited. I took a friend with me. She had complained of demonic problems, and the drive would give us time to discuss how to pursue her freedom. The trip was a true memory-maker because of something amazing that happened.

There was fresh snow on the ground as we entered the town, such a pretty sight. After servicing the location in need of chemicals, Lara and I got into my van for the two hour drive back to Visalia. The temperature was around 35 degrees.

Naturally, I turned on the heater. As we drove out of town, the van became uncomfortably hot in the cold weather. I turned off the heater, but it was still hot in the van. Lara said the heat was coming from my body. All the way home it was hot in the van. The heater was never needed.

When we arrived at her apartment, unusual warmth continued to emit from me as we went inside. We had been inside for a few minutes when something strange happened. She decided to lie on the living room floor as we talked about her promiscuous lifestyle and demonic problems.

What happened next was unexpected. Suddenly, while talking about her problem, her mouth opened wide and a stream of dark air came out of it. Sometimes the air was consistently black, and other times there were breaks in the dark stream. During this time, she was pinned to the floor. I realized the Holy Spirit was driving out demons. This continued for about a minute.

She could not close her mouth until the demons were out of her. We talked about what happened, and she was relieved to have the demons out of her. It was not revealed how the demons got in her body.

Teaching: When reaching out to help demonized people, you cannot predict in each case exactly how the Holy Spirit will overpower the enemy. In 35 years of helping people, I have never experienced this heat again.

*Case 9: Demonic Healings With Rose Petals

Jesus sent a new friend into my life, a man I met at a Bible study. We connected quickly. When he found out I had helped people with demonic problems, he shared some spiritual problems in his life. I spent time counseling with him, and it was determined that a relative of his had used an evil spirit for healing. He was open to the fact that the evil spirit had been passed down in the family. At times, Trace felt the evil presence in his house, and members of his family sensed it too.

This healing lady used rose petals for getting the attention of a specific spirit to do healing or cast spells. As a recent convert to Christ, Trace was convinced his relative's power to heal was not from Jesus. We were sitting at the kitchen table as he renounced the demon activity passed down to him. He began to shake and said "Can you feel it. The devil's here!"

The demonic presence around him was obvious. It looked like thick heat waves were pulling away from his body. Within seconds, the outer oppression that had irritated Trace for years was gone. He continues to be a faithful servant of Jesus, a solid Christian, and a close friend.

Teaching: This was a case of generational demon activity passed down to a grandson who knew nothing about it. When he became a Christian, the Holy Spirit began to help him realize an evil presence was in his house. Sometimes relatives use evil spirits in rituals and the innocent have the evil presence passed on to them. Also, a dream catcher, given to his son from a woman in the occult, was found and destroyed.

*Case 10: Drug Use Allowed Demons to Enter

This adult man had a history of drug use. He had smoked marijuana, hash, dropped acid (LSD), taken Mescaline, and taken speed pills. He had become a Christian, was experiencing emotional problems, and was having trouble focusing on his relationship with Jesus.

During counseling, it was obvious that he saw the sin of illegal drug use in his life. As he repented and confessed his sin, I saw demons come out of his head. The demons were gone in less than a minute.

Teaching: Drug use is common in the occult for the purpose of altering the mind, which allows demons to enter the person. When mixed, drugs and demonic sensations cause a person to experience a new euphoria. Upon deliverance from evil, this man's spiritual relationship with Jesus immediately improved and Bible reading became easier. The fact that the demons came out of his head indicates where they were functioning to cause deception.

*Case 11: A Fast Food Repentance

A pastor and I had been working with a woman, and it was frustrating at times, because we kept encountering resistant demonic strongholds. It seemed more difficult than usual to cast out demons when they surfaced and spoke through the woman. The next day, the lady and I met for lunch at a well-known fast food restaurant.

As we discussed her progress, something important came to my mind. The previous night I had tried to force a demon to give me information that was none of my spiritual business. I realized this was a sin, and told her I was wrong in trying to force a demon to give hidden information that was not God's will.

I told the lady that I needed to confess my sin of Spiritism because of my unneeded conversation with the evil spirit. As I finished my sentence, her face changed and a demon yelled out of her mouth "No!" Quickly I repented of my sin, and the demon left our lunch time. Later I told the pastor what had happened.

Teaching: Don't be impatient when dealing with stubborn demons who are hard to cast out. Fasting and more prayer are needed (Matthew 17:21). It is also common to see demons cast out in public than most people believe. If you read the Gospels, Jesus cast out demons in the public, synagogues, and houses. Let's follow Christ's example.

*Case 12: The Woman Was Deceived

I left for Chico, California, to visit a friend. He had expressed concern for the wife of a close friend. She was convinced that if she lost her strong faith, all of Chico would fall to the devil. She believed Jesus had told her that the entire town of Chico would stand or fall spiritually according to her faith. This was a clear case of demonic, delusional deception.

For weeks, her husband had tried to persuade her that the town did not rest on one person's faith. There were many steadfast Christians in Chico at this time. Thus, God would not let Satan take over this town by ignoring their faith.

As I talked to her, she was gentle but defiant in giving up her belief. She was convinced that she had heard from God on this issue. In a few days, I was on my way home wondering what the outcome of her deception would bring. Later I was told the marriage ended in divorce, and Chico did not fall under satanic rule.

Teaching: There was no Scripture to support her belief, but that did not matter to her. This proves the depth of her false belief. Any time a person claims to have heard specific instructions from the LORD, it must not contradict any Scripture. Her deception destroyed her marriage.

Case 13: She Stuck Pins in the Baby's Feet

My mother called me and seemed a little nervous as she began talking to me. Within a minute, I knew why. She told me she thought this young teenager at a relative's house had a demon in her. I asked my mother to explain why she thought this girl had a demon in her. She said:

> "When Susan sees the picture of Jesus in the hallway, she spits on it. And she has been sticking pins in the baby's feet, making her cry. Her grandmother and I talked to her about it. She denies hurting the baby, but we have seen the marks on the baby's feet from the pins she used. Also, her grandmother and I have been choked by an invisible force since Susan came to visit. Do you think she's demon-possessed?"

We talked about prayer for Susan. I told my mother the facts she had revealed indicated Susan had demonic problems, and that I would pray and get back to her. Immediately I was grieved in my spirit as I spent time in prayer, seeking God's wisdom. My main concern was that Susan did not remember sticking pins in the baby's feet. This sounded like a demonic trance would overcome her and block out the evil she was doing.

That night the Lord Jesus was very gracious to me. He gave me a dream which showed me and a friend how we would be helping Susan. In the dream, I saw the exact face of the girl I would see a few days later. The dream showed us telling her about Jesus and how she could receive Him as her Lord and Savior. Suddenly she looked at my fish symbol in a cross on a necklace I was wearing. The blue in her eyes changed to black. Then her throat began to swell as the indwelling demon began choking her. Quickly I said: "In the Name of Jesus release her and come out of her!" The demon came out of her and the dream ended, and "exact reality" was a few days away.

I called my mom the next day and told her to let the lady know I would make plans to travel to help Susan. My drive would be a little over an hour from where I lived. My cousin lived in the town where I would travel to help the young girl. He knew the lady and was welcome in her home. As a Christian of dedicated faith, he was ready to help with the deliverance.

When God guides, God provides. I called the lady to set up a time of prayer for the girl. The grandmother was a widow. She thought her son would approve and gave us permission to pray for her granddaughter.

When we arrived, I saw Susan. She looked exactly like the girl I had seen in my dream, verifying the LORD had given it to me. We talked for a few minutes and the grandmother was asked to leave for a couple of hours. Her grandmother and my mom had previously taken some time to prepare Susan for our arrival. The three of us sat in the living room and I began to ask Susan questions about any unusual things that were happening in her life or what might be troubling her at any time.

She said that every night the curtains would blow back and forth in her room, even when the window was closed. Low tone voices were sometimes heard, and she had to have a light on to sleep. The darkness scared her. As she told us these things, she began to tremble, and we knew the demons were getting ready to defend their invasion.

We had been talking about the Lord Jesus to her for a few minutes. Suddenly, the demons started to move her away from us. They were commanded to stop and they took her to the carpet in convulsions. We began to pray and rebuke the demons. She had more than one in her. As they came out, we came face to face with the final (main) demon, also called the strongman.

Susan sat up and looked around in a type of trance state. The entire iris in both of her eyes was now black and glared with hatred at me and my cousin. The LORD directed her eyes toward my chain which had a cross inside of a fish symbol. It was dangling toward her. Immediately the demon saw my necklace and began choking her. Just like in the dream God gave me, her throat began to bloat and swell. She couldn't talk.

Quickly I said: "Release her in the Name of Jesus and come out of her!" Within a few seconds, the Holy Spirit drove the evil spirit out of her. She looked at me and cried out: "It left me!" Her countenance, and her eyes came back to normal. We told her about the Gospel of Jesus, His love, and desire to forgive her sins. She understood her problem with sin and prayed for Jesus to forgive her and come into her life as Lord and Savior. Her face now had a peaceful countenance.

Grandma came back and saw a new granddaughter. A few days later, I checked back with Susan and here is what she told me: "The night I prayed to ask Jesus into my life was peaceful. The curtains did not blow around. I did not hear any voices in the night, and I slept with the lights off. I got some rest. Thank you for helping me."

When Susan went back home and her parents heard about her deliverance and conversion to Christ, the enemy was already at work in them. They were upset about the deliverance and here is why: The father was an agnostic and was married to a Native American "wild woman."

The mother had an erratic behavior reputation. There was no evidence she had ever renounced the spiritual powers she inherited from her tribal ancestors. The occult sins were passed down to the daughter without Susan knowing it (Exodus 20:5). However, Jesus set her free, but problems were looming in the future.

Susan's parents did not support her decision to follow Christ, and she was not encouraged to get involved with any church for spiritual growth in Jesus. Living at home in an atmosphere of Biblical rejection and witchcraft tore her down. Eventually she went back into the world of sin, which included sexual immorality, drug use, not spending time reading her Bible, and setting Jesus aside. Her drug use led her to time in prison. I have not heard from her in over 30 years, but I still pray for her.

Teaching: This was my first exposure in helping someone with demonic problems, and I was ignorant concerning the importance of immediate discipleship for the new convert. Also, it is always wise to get parental permission when praying for a minor. Her grandmother took the verbal heat from the girl's father, but was not sorry Jesus had helped Susan. And, it is wise to have a woman present when men are praying for another woman. This protects the reputation of all who are ministering, because demons can plant lies in a "trance demoniac" and make the person believe and say improper touches occurred when they did not.

Case 14: Fighting Damien, the Son of Lucifer

I shared with some friends how the Lord Jesus had set Susan free. Within a few months Jack talked to me about a concern a girl named Tonya had shared with him. She had a friend who had been through counseling for depression and emotional trauma. Lindy was getting worse, yet she had received Jesus as her Lord and Savior months earlier. Tonya wondered if her friend might have a demonic problem. A time was set up to introduce me to Lindy.

In prayer, I drove to Lindy's apartment where Tonya was waiting. As I entered and was introduced to Lindy, I noticed she avoided sustained eye contact. This is common when people are demon-indwelled, but doesn't always indicate a person has a demon in them. We talked for a few minutes about her increasing spiritual struggles since she had become a Christian. She was becoming more uneasy as we talked about what her problem might be that "basic Christian counseling" couldn't help. By basic, I mean counseling that does not discern for demons in a person's life.

Then the Holy Spirit directed me to give her a Bible and have her read 1 John 1:7 which reads:

> But if we walk in the light, as He is in the light, we have
> fellowship one with another, and the blood of Jesus Christ His
> Son cleanseth us from all sin.

Lindy began to slightly tremble as she read the word "light." When she got to the word "blood," she began to shake with convulsions, could not read anymore, and the Bible nearly fell out of her lap as she went into a short trance. She did not remember all that had transpired while reading the verse. I took the Bible and told Tonya I knew what the problem was with her friend.

I did not tell Lindy that she had a demon in her. I never tell the person in advance they are "demon-indwelled" if I know it, because the evil spirits can begin to call for strong reinforcements of resistance. But I did mention there seemed to be a demonic problem in her life that needed prayer. I told Lindy we needed to set up a time to go through her dozens of books to discard any linked to the occult realm. She agreed and a few days later Jack came with me to throw out books. There were shelves of books, but it was essential because evil spirits like evil literature (Acts 19:19-20).

Now, the battle was beginning to become intense. As we loaded many books into boxes, one of the boxes began to make thumping and banging sounds. The demons were trying to distract us. We prayed and she asked us to take all of her books except her Bible. This definitely confirmed she was willing to do whatever it took to be set free from demons.

Lindy told us there was an occult-referenced paper she had written about the World War II Nazi SS Troops that had to be found and destroyed. We found it, and a demon yelled and shook her repeatedly as we ripped it to pieces.

We drove to a park where we could burn her numerous books of secular and occult content that "exalted itself against the knowledge of God" (2 Corinthians 10:5). We placed them in a 50 gallon drum and began to burn them. At times, we heard demons screaming out of the flames in rage. We watched and prayed until every wicked book was in ashes (Acts 19:18-20).

With her permission, I kept one book. It was her diary and contained valuable information. She had recorded the day she repented, received Christ, and was born-again months earlier. At this time in my Christian walk, I was convinced a Christian could not have a demon in their body. Yet Lindy had recorded that "after" she became a Christian, her depression increased and her life was more confusing. A specific entry captivated my attention: "Lord it seems like every time I take one step to You, I fall two steps backward. Why?"

This diary entry moved me to seek an accurate understanding of the Greek structure in the Gospel demonic accounts, because the Greek opens the door to better knowledge. Within months, I would revise my position of "It's not possible for a demon to enter a Christian" to, "If a Christian opens the spiritual door for a demon, the demon will enter."

We had to set up a place and time for Lindy's deliverance from evil spirits. A friend told me of a Christian couple who had a foothill country house and had prayed for people with demonic problems. I phoned them and they wanted to support Lindy's deliverance at their house. A couple of days later, Lindy, Tonya, Jack, and I drove to their house, and our lives would never be the same because of the explosive demonic resistance.

When the four of us arrived, Lindy was very nervous as soon as she got out of the car. She would not go inside the house and walked around the property enjoying the scenery. We had to be patient and trust in the LORD. It took at least 10 minutes of prayer away from her and persuasive talk to calm her down and convince her to go in the house. The demons knew the battle for her freedom was to begin in the house.

As we got comfortable in the front room and began to talk, the demons started making her tremble. Quickly she slouched to the floor, completely unconscious. We began to pray for her, asking the LORD to drive out the evil spirits. Suddenly a demon began raging and screaming at us. I began to rebuke it and commanded it to leave. For almost two hours we prayed and rebuked the demons, commanding them to leave in the Name of Jesus! Some demons left, but the final intensity of the battle was ahead.

Lindy became conscious, was exhausted, and her throat was so sore she could barely speak. We prayed and decided to stop and take her home to finish the deliverance the next day in Jack's house. Lindy knew the spiritual battle would be more intense at the end because of a powerful demon still lodged in her. At her apartment, Tonya stayed with her, and she got some sleep.

We set up another prayer session, picked up Lindy and went to Jack's house. It was easier to get her in the house for prayer this time. Quickly the demons had her on the floor thrashing and yelling through her. We prayed, called upon the LORD, and rebuked the demon activity. There was one demon that was more vicious than the others. As he continued to scream out, I said "In the Name of Jesus, who are you!" This was his response: "I am Damien, the son of Lucifer! I will follow you and kill you!" We ignored the threat, rebuked Damien, and continued the deliverance. Years later, Damien would try to fulfill his threat to me.

After more than an hour, we could tell Damien's resistance and roaring were weakening. Oh, did we rejoice that the end was near. We reminded Damien that Lindy had chosen Jesus as her Lord and Savior, and she had rejected him. Finally Damien was commanded again to leave Lindy in Jesus' Name. He left her and the room was very quiet. The peace of God greeted all of us. Almost two hours had passed. We thanked the Lord Jesus and prayed.

That same week Lindy was being discipled by me and two Christian ladies. The church I was attending was gracious to help her financially and did not require her to attend their church. The pastors at my church supported my work in deliverance with prayer and encouragement. Their concern was that she lock into a church with understanding and support of her ferocious battle for spiritual freedom.

With a friend, Lindy found a congregation for spiritual growth. She had been living alone, but her new helping friend was also a single lady so they moved into a nice two bedroom apartment. Now Lindy had a smile I had not seen before. Jesus set her free and her new roommate was a quality Christian of compassion who understood spiritual warfare. When God guides, God provides.

Teaching: Sometimes a deliverance can take more than one prayer session. Fasting and praying in advance for the day of a known deliverance is advised for Holy Spirit guidance. Make sure all involved are not in any sin. Allow the Holy Spirit to choose the site for the deliverance. When completed, check on the person weekly to see if oppression has returned. Pray as led by the Holy Spirit (Ephesians 6:18). For several months, I saw Lindy and watched her grow in love and knowledge. Then the two of them moved to work in another town. God bless them forever. They are the kind of people I want to be around in Heaven — forever!

There is another fact you should know. In Lindy's apartment before she was set free, Damien said to me: "I know of you." What did this mean? Susan was the only demonized person I had ever prayed for, and that was in a town over 60 miles from Fresno. When you cast out demons, they circulate your name as "a marked target" to their evil spirit brothers. Years later, while near Portland, Oregon, Damien crossed state lines to make an attempt to disrupt my counsel for a woman who needed deliverance.

Case 15: The Witch Wanted Help for Her Baby

Robert, a Christian friend, called me and said a practicing witch he used to spend time with had phoned him with a concern. Carla knew of Robert's occult background and also knew that he had become a Christian. She told him her daughter, who was less than two years old, was being bothered by an evil spirit. She was active in her rituals, but nothing she did kept her little girl always protected at night. Carla asked for help for her daughter.

When Robert gave me the details, I said I would help. Our main focus would be on getting Carla to renounce her witchcraft (confess her sin) and call upon Jesus for salvation. We would also pray for her child. Before we set up a time to meet with Carla, Robert told me that she was adept at curses and spells. With this knowledge, my prayers were for Jesus to protect us from any demonic interference.

We met in the afternoon at her apartment. She began by telling us that her daughter had been having more trouble sleeping. Her disrupted sleep patterns were getting worse and were accompanied with sudden cries of pain. Carla was also being afflicted with problems. She said red rashes would appear suddenly on her arms, increase in size for a while, and would slowly fade away. Nothing she tried with her occult knowledge put a permanent stop to these physical problems.

I talked to her about Jesus' Gospel and His power to prevent the evil spirits from harming her and her daughter. Carla was not yet ready to surrender her life to Jesus. Disappointed, I continued to talk about Jesus. From the bedroom, her daughter was suddenly awakened with a loud cry.

Robert and I knew the demons were mad at our presence with the Gospel. Prayer for the child relaxed her back to sleep.

Suddenly red spots began appearing and expanding on both of Carla's arms. We watched as they increased. Then I told Carla Jesus has power over the devil and his demons to prevent the red rashes. She just looked at me and let it happen. What I told her next had to be prompted by the Holy Spirit, because I had never said anything like it before and have not since. I told her she could tell the demon causing the rashes to "Stop it in the Name of Jesus!" She did this, and in less than thirty seconds the rashes had disappeared. Her child now had rashes appearing on her. I told Carla to command the demon to stop it. She did and quickly the rashes were gone.

I explained to Carla that all her occult knowledge and power had been of no help to her. She had seen the power of Jesus remove the rashes that were on her and on her child. Continuing to establish the importance of receiving Christ to forgive her sins and provide protection from further demonic physical assaults still did not convince her to accept Christ as her Lord and Savior.

Another idea came to my mind. I thought about how Jesus reaches out to us with open arms of love. Standing up, I extended my arms with open palms to her, and told her how Jesus extends his love to her. She looked at my hands with surprised eyes and said the following: "I see the stigmata in your hands!" This stunned all of us. She did not see blood coming out of my hands, only pierced marks.

Again we explained her immediate need for Jesus, but she would not renounce and give up all of her occult powers. Proving to be a fool, she wanted both Christ's and Satan's power. She had seen that Christ's cleansing rash power was superior to the devil's affliction rash power, but was blind to the Gospel, proving the reality of 2 Corinthians 4:4.

If you are thinking that "an unbeliever" can't use the Name of Jesus against a demonic illness, then find a Scripture in proper context proving your position (Matthew 7:22-23). While you are looking, remember that before we were saved, the Holy Spirit was at work to bring us as sinners to repentance. Pharaoh was *not* a true follower of the LORD when he was given "two dreams of grace" from the LORD (Genesis 41:1-5).

Who is the LORD's counselor that he should tell the Almighty God what to do in any situation? (Romans 11:34). As for showing Carla the stigmata in my hands, that is His business. It has happened only once in my forty-four years as a servant of the Lord Jesus. Perhaps in the future, Carla will read Galatians 2:20 where Paul talks about being "crucified with Christ," and this will bring her to salvation.

Teaching: For me, it is so disturbing that Jesus would do amazing signs to convince Carla to repent and choose the bright and powerful side of abundant and eternal life, and then she would not respond to His love. Apparently she cared more about keeping demonic power in her life for control of chosen situations (she liked being lord of her life), rather than keeping her child protected from evil. I told her we were available if she wanted to talk more about Jesus. She never called.

Maybe Luke 17:11-19 can shed more understanding on why Carla did not want Christ in her life. Ten lepers were healed, but only one turned back to give God the glory and give Jesus thanks (verses 15-16). The others wanted their social life back, and to them running to town was more important than giving glory to God and thanking the Lord.

We don't know what else we could have done. We prepared with prayer, presented the Gospel more than once, prayed for her child, and she saw the healing power of Jesus over Satan. But it was not to be as we had prayed and hoped for (Ecclesiastes 3:1).

Case 16: A Desperate Mother's Plea for Help

The peace in my apartment was interrupted by the phone. A woman, who attended my home church, had called the pastor for help with her Christian son who was now working at an occult bookstore. A pastor gave her my phone number. It was a blessing to attend a congregation where the pastors had confidence in my efforts to help those with demonic problems. Their support was a source of strength for me.

She explained that her son, Arnold, had been attending church on a regular basis and had moved out of the house. When she did not see him at church on a consistent schedule, she called him to see if all was well. She was shocked to hear him say he had a job working in an occult bookstore.

Her concerns were important, because he did not want to meet with her to talk about his new job. Her appeal was desperate for me to go to the occult book store to talk to her son and make sure he was okay physically, because she knew spiritually he was not well.

I told her I would go to the store to talk to her son to let him know his mother loved him and just wanted to see him for conversation. Prayer preparation began for wisdom, protection, and that her son would be open for conversation. This was a new outreach for me, and I was eager to serve Jesus to help a loving mother. I drove to downtown Fresno and parked by the store, praying again before I entered the place of demon activity.

I was greeted by the manager behind the counter and he said to me: "You're a Christian, aren't you? I could feel it when you came in the store." I asked if Arnold was working, while taking time to explain that his mother had not seen him or heard from him in over a week. He directed me to the back room where Arnold was arranging books on shelves. I introduced myself to Arnold and told him about his mother's concerns. We talked for a while, and he said he would call his mother, which he did within a few days.

As I was leaving the store, the manager said that I was the *only* Christian who had ever entered his store and didn't start rebuking demons. We began to talk about how he got involved with running an occult bookstore. He told me his grandfather and father were both ministers, but were hypocrites. Growing up in this disappointing atmosphere, he rebelled, left home, and eventually became a manager of his own occult bookstore.

The Lord Jesus had given me the privilege of acceptance from this man in a demonic place to help Arnold (Matthew 18:12-14). He said I was welcome to come back anytime if I wanted to, but I was never directed by the Holy Spirit to go back. My mission was to find Arnold and get him to call his mother. Arnold called her and they met. She persuaded him to leave his occult job and move back home.

A week later, they were in church. I prayed for Arnold, but his recovery from outer oppression was a slow process. There was no evidence he was indwelled by a demon. For weeks his eyes had a glassy look, and his desire to once again read the Bible and grow in his relationship with Jesus were inconsistent. Arnold didn't realize that working in an occult bookstore could have lingering complications.

Teaching: As I evaluated his slow progress, I realized his constant work at the occult bookstore had exposed him to strong demon activity daily that did not want to give up control over his life. Both Arnold and his mother should have prayed together more often, asking the LORD to break all demonic strongholds that he let come into his life. My prayers for them also should have been more frequent. He broke contact with the manager, and to my knowledge he did not bring any occult items (books) home.

Case 17: Demons Entered Her in a Pentagram

A friend named Don was a student at Fresno State, majoring in Journalism. He was interested in my demonic encounters. One of his class assignments was to interview someone in a controversial area and write it up. Don asked me if I would do an interview with him on demon-possession for his assignment. I agreed.

As we talked, I gave him explicit details of my recent encounters with people who sought my help from demonic control. Don was captivated by the information I shared with him about my explosive battle with Damien, the Son of Lucifer. We focused on the details, and he submitted the paper to his teacher. His Journalism instructor liked it and asked Don to talk with me about giving a class presentation on demon-possession. I agreed.

Within two weeks, I was at the front of his Journalism class presenting my first prayer session with a demoniac and also my explosive encounter with a demon named Damien, who had claimed to be Lucifer's son. After about 30 minutes of details on demons, I opened it up for questions. All the students were open to the fact that demon-possession was real in our world. They wanted to know how demons enter people and if demonic cases were common. I gave them answers to all their questions. When time ran out for the class period, they were polite with applause.

The classroom discussion of this subject quickly circulated around the campus, and the campus newspaper wanted to publish an article that covered my Journalism class presentation. Don got back to me, and we went over various details that we believed were essential for the campus article. In a few weeks the title, *One Man's Lonely Fight Against Evil*, was read by hundreds of Fresno State students. Details on spiritual warfare were printed to give readers an idea on how demons study and invade people. Because of this information, my life would change soon.

People called me to comment on the campus article. But when one specific call came through from a woman named Joan, I knew I was again going to be facing demons in a person. The student sounded shy, hesitant, and very nervous during the conversation while mentioning her occult involvement. She had read the article and felt she might have demons in her and wanted to meet with me. We agreed to meet at a restaurant at 7 pm two days later.

When the time came, I drove to the restaurant praying during my drive for the Holy Spirit to fill me, protect me from demons, and discernment to help her. As I walked to the front entrance, something critical came to my thoughts. I asked the LORD to protect my mind and not allow her to know anything I was thinking. This was a vital prayer.

Some Christians believe that when you are in sin, your thoughts are not protected and certain demons can hear your thoughts. Others believe that it is impossible for a demon to read your mind or hear your thoughts at any time. I don't argue about this issue. We can hear our thoughts, so there must be a "decibel thought level" of some type. Since thoughts produce sound, maybe they can be heard in the spirit realm. Therefore, it is wise to pray for Christ's protection. Perhaps, if we are in sin, it does allow certain demons to hear our thoughts. One thing I do know; when you ask the LORD to guard your mind, He will.

Upon entering the restaurant, I looked at some booths and in one there was a lady by herself. I walked toward her. Joan smiled and we exchanged names. Immediately I felt spiritually uncomfortable and was thankful I had prayed a lot before this meeting.

As I sat across from her, I could feel the demon activity that was in her. The evil spirits were looking through her eyes at me. When I talk to demonic people, I try to look at their eyebrows most of the time when I see that an evil spirit is looking through their eyes. This helps me to relax and stay better focused on our discussion, because sometimes a quick flash of a darkness in a pair of soft blue eyes can be disruptive in gathering facts.

After about 10 minutes of discussion as to why she thought she had a demonic problem, she made a statement which confirmed some of her witchcraft power. Here is what Joan said:

"I can't believe it. I can't believe it. You are the first person
I've ever sat down with, and I can't know your thoughts."

Immediately I remembered the prayer for mind and thought protection I had prayed before I entered the restaurant. God is faithful to watch over His people. During the remainder of our conversation, she told me that she had been initiated in the occult in Texas. The details of her "free-will" initiation included (1) standing in a Pentagram circle to open her soul to Satan for power and (2) allowing a specific demon to enter her while she was in the demonic circle with other demonized people watching. This information also made me aware that other demons had entered her as she continued to meet with her devoted demon-worshippers until she left Texas.

Tactfully I ended the conversation. I had heard enough to know this would be a violent, spirit-raging confrontation when the time came to pray for her freedom from various indwelling demons. Most likely it would take multiple prayer sessions to complete her deliverance and ongoing spiritual healing would be needed (Luke 4:18).

A few days later with friends, we met at a church to start the deliverance. One mistake we made was that we didn't have her verbally renounce "in detail" all of her occult involvement. Her confession of sin had been somewhat casual. If a demonized person is sincerely repentant during renunciation of all occult sins, demons sometimes try to choke them, make them shake, drop them to the floor, or cause them to go unconscious. When any of these demonic manifestations occur, the demons responsible for these actions are firmly commanded to "Stop it and leave in the Name of Jesus!" If you are operating in the authority and power of the Holy Spirit, demons will leave.

Quickly we were facing demons speaking through her, yelling, and resisting our command to "Come out of her in the Name of Jesus!" We made progress, but soon realized she had many demons to confront so another deliverance session was set up and more demons were cast out.

Joan had asked me to attend her church a few days after our first prayer session to meet the pastor of the college and career group where she attended. I met him, and he was happy that Joan was getting help for what he considered her "traumatic emotional problems." He had no idea she was demon-indwelled.

During the service, she took Communion, as it was called at her church. A demon manifested as she drank the cup which represented Christ's cleansing blood for our sins and said: "It burrrns!" There was no demonic explosion to disrupt the service. As we walked out Joan wanted to spit on a life-size picture of Jesus, but didn't. She was visibly irritated as we left the church, but no demons were cast out of her that night.

Again we met and cast out more demons. We decided to tape this encounter (she consented) for verifying any questions Joan might have about her times of being unconscious. Recorded demonic confrontations can be helpful in training others and convincing some about the vicious, invisible spiritual realm of evil spirits. Discretion should be used when playing recorded demonic encounters to teach those about spiritual warfare who were not at the deliverance session.

Joan was seeing a Christian counselor at this time to treat her for depression and suicidal thoughts. He had noticed improvement in her countenance, for she would now look at his face more during discussions. He asked her what had occurred to help her gain this change for the better. She told him about her occult background for the first time, and said Christians had cast demons out of her. Her counselor did not like what he heard. Since he believed she was a Christian, he rejected her explanation for her improvement. He exploded and told her that she didn't have a demonic problem.

She looked at him and said: "My friends taped what happened and you can listen to it." Then he really got angry and asked for my name and phone number. Depressed, she called me after her counseling session and told me what the counselor had said. He wanted the tapes immediately given to her so she could give them to him for destruction, and if I didn't give him the tapes he would pursue legal action. He had no desire to listen to the tapes for proof. She came by and took the tapes to him.

This misguided Christian counselor has a doctorate and heads a major counseling service in central California. He wouldn't even meet with me or take time to listen to the tapes privately. His defiant response to rejecting improvement through prayer and casting out demons is more common than Christians realize. Such an attitude does not offer the patient the fullness of Christ's love and understanding. Too many counselors scorn the obvious demonic attack against humanity that was earlier described in the chapter titled *Scriptures That Teach Demon Activity*.

Demons can't be "counseled out" of a person. They will listen to the misleading, insufficient psychological advice and warp it in the person's mind. Demons must be rebuked "In the Name of Jesus" and commanded to leave the person. Holy Spirit led counseling uses *only* the Scripture to counsel the broken-hearted and "to preach deliverance to the captives" (Luke 4:18). This truth sets the captives free (John 8:31-32).

True Holy Spirit-led counseling strengthens a person to become a fruit-bearing Christian (John 15:8; Galatians 5:22-23), whereas secular counseling may help at times but still leaves the demonized vulnerable to ongoing demonic affliction. It's hard to find a Bible college or Christian university that only uses the Word of God for recovery and counseling.

Psychology degrees without a Genesis to Revelation understanding of demonic spiritual warfare are not sufficient to "completely help" all who come for help. The Bible is God's gift to us for the best possible guidance, healing, and removal (treating) of any demonic affliction, or any problem. Colossians 2:8 warns us about "philosophy and vain deceit after the traditions of men." Christians should not believe that the philosophies and psychological teachings from man's viewpoints are sharper (better) than the two-edged sword of the Holy Spirit, which is the Word of God (Ephesians 6:17). God's Scripture is inspired (2 Timothy 3:16-17). Books with "man's philosophies and psychology" are not God-inspired.

Joan still wanted our help. I told her we would continue praying for her. Apparently, her counselor forgot to tell her not to see us for more prayer. Joan came to my apartment where other friends were waiting as prayer support. We had her read a verse that included the word "light." When she would get to this word, she would not read it. She read as if this word (light) was not printed on the page. We then asked the LORD to remove any demon activity that was blinding her from reading the verse and open her eyes to read the entire verse.

Now, when Joan read the same verse again and read the word "light," a demon screamed out of her and left. The demon had been blocking her vision from seeing Jesus as "the true light of the world." She had been initiated into a demonic Pentagram of darkness, and the demons hated the light of Christ (John 8:12). More demons were cast out of her that evening, but we weren't done.

After the session, a friend brought an important fact to my attention. She had never asked us to come to her residence where she stayed with her grandmother. When a person is seeking deliverance from evil spirits, they must allow the prayer team to enter their residence to remove and destroy all occult objects. Before we could do this, the evil presence around my apartment was becoming intense. It was so bad I could feel it when I got to within 10 feet of my door.

I prayed that the LORD would protect me with "the blood" like He did for His people in Egypt during the time of Moses. Specifically, I asked Him to make the frame of my door look blood red to the demons and drive them away. A few days later, my prayer was answered in a powerful way. Chuck and I were in my apartment discussing Joan's demonic situation when someone knocked on my door. It was Joan. She was nervous wanted to talk.

As she stood on my porch, her eyes looked at my door frame and she said: "When did you get your door frame painted red?" Then she looked up at the front of my apartment and said: "The whole front of your apartment is red!" and passed out in my doorway. She was completely unconscious. There is power and protection in the blood of Jesus! We couldn't awaken her and had to make a decision. Do we leave her in the doorway and wait for her to become conscious?

Our decision was unusual. We grabbed each of her wrists and began to sing a Maranatha Praise 2 song titled "Sing Hallelujah." The demons screamed in rage in the doorway, so we took her inside and proceeded to cast out some demons. When finished, we knew we had to go to her residence to check for any occult objects she might have kept before continuing the deliverance. We talked with Joan and she agreed to have us come to her house.

Chuck and I went to her residence. We found over a dozen statues of owl pairs. This was serious, because the owl is the symbol of wisdom in the occult, and Joan had contact with an evil spirit of wisdom indwelling her. Chuck brought to my attention that when Joan was in a full demonic trance, her face looked like an owl and her body bloated to take the shape of an owl. This gave us insight to cast out any demons that were involved with giving her the appearance of an owl.

We told her she would have to destroy the owls that she used for occult wisdom, but she did not. Now we knew there was reason to believe she would not surrender all to Jesus for complete deliverance, and we began to seek Christ's wisdom as to continue with her or not. Our answer would come within a few weeks.

One morning at 10 o'clock, Joan came to my apartment to talk without first phoning me. She was depressed and told me some of the demons had reentered her the previous night. I asked her to tell me what she did to allow some demons back into her. She said they told her they would no longer help her to get the grades in her college education she needed to be a hospital administrator. So she let them back in for a well-paying job with prestige.

My attention was drawn to Luke 4:5-8 where the Devil tempted Jesus with power and authority to control people. Hospital administrators have substantial power and authority over many people. Satan had found her weak point, and she trusted in Satan for a job rather than the Lord Jesus. We spent time talking about her lack of commitment to repentance. I told her she would need to find someone else to finish her deliverance.

She was angry and went to the pastor at my home church. After listening to her complaint and knowing me well, Joan was advised to seek help elsewhere. It is vital to have staff support with their spiritual authority upon you when you are dealing directly with demonic cases. Because of her rebellion, the prayer team severed all contact from her (Matthew 7:6).

On one occasion, when we were praying and casting out demons in my apartment, the demons used her to call and harass us. When I picked up the phone, I heard heavy, ugly breathing like I had heard during her deliverance sessions. We prayed for Jesus to block any demons she was sending to interfere with the demonized person seeking help.

One more thing should be mentioned to show how we sought to help her with patience and love. During a time of discussion at a table, a demon took over her completely and was glaring at me. It pulled a long knife out of her purse with the intent to ram it in me. In my mind, I called upon the

LORD to protect me. It was a stare down for a while. Jesus prevented the demon from using her to harm me. Out of her trance, she was shocked to find that she had this knife in her possession.

Teaching: Before praying for any one coming out of the occult where they did a ritual for power (Pentagram or Hexagram with a circle of demon-indwelled friends), make them destroy all objects (athame-occult knife for blood rituals, clothing, books, candles, chalice, crystals, etc.) connected in any way to demons. If people seeking deliverance are sincere, they will tell you what objects are evil in their house. Also, ask them about any verbal contract made with demons for power, wealth, or prestige.

Have them slowly and carefully renounce every form of occult involvement. If they are attending a congregation, notify the pastor so that prayer is constant from those in authority. After each prayer session, let them know of the progress. Pray that the demon activity in the person would not be allowed to cause problems in the church service. Ask Jesus to open the ears, mind, and heart of the demonic person when reading the Bible and listening to *gentle*, heart-healing Christian music. People with demonic problems don't need wild contemporary music of any kind. And remember, witches do send demons to hinder deliverance sessions. This has happened to us more than once.

Case 18: Instant Phone Healing For a Demoniac

The information about this miraculous physical healing is linked to Joan, the demonized lady from Texas we spent months trying to help. During the weeks of counsel, prayers, and casting out demons, she developed a severe ear infection that caused her entire left jaw and cheek to swell. She was being treated with strong antibiotics, but the infection would not respond to any medication.

She called me one night to tell me her doctor wanted to see her in the morning to schedule surgery on her infected and plugged ear. Knowing that evil spirits of infirmity and sickness are common in Satan's arsenal of suffering, I told her that I would like to pray for her healing and cast out any demon responsible for her infection. She agreed and this is what happened for God's glory.

Joan was silent for about 5 seconds. Then the voice of a demon spoke through her mouth and said these words to me: "I made her sick with the infection. I will take away the sickness if you let me stay in her, and I will not make her sick again. Don't cast me out." Demons are liars and will afflict people in various ways when indwelling them.

Over the phone, I commanded the demon to "Come out of her in the Name of Jesus!" Immediately she was thrown to the floor. How do I know this? In the background, I could hear her banging into furniture as the demon fought to stay in her. Suddenly it was quiet. Then she picked up the phone and told me, "A chuck of wax just popped out of my ear, and the infection is draining!" She ended our conversation. Despite her abundance of sin, Jesus showed healing mercy.

The next day Joan went to see her doctor. As he examined her, he was in awe. In all his years of practice, he had never seen a serious ear infection heal overnight like this one did. The surgery was cancelled. However, weeks later we would find that this miraculous healing from Jesus was not received with a repentant heart of thanksgiving leading to full repentance. We continued to counsel and pray for Joan, but eventually she chose the world and took her concealed issues to another church.

Teaching: Sometimes instant healings do not bring all to repentance and true devotion to Jesus as recorded in Luke 17:11-18. The Gospels include several accounts of sickness induced by evil spirits. Demons work around the clock to send fiery darts and missiles of oppression to Christians (Ephesians 6:16). When we receive demonic lies in our heads, it can eventually cause spiritual, emotional, or exhaustive physical problems. Our immune systems, both physical and spiritual, can become weak. Then sickness plants itself in our life for a time. Also, remember that you don't have to be in the presence of a person to cast out a demon. Prayers, as well as commands, are heard in the spiritual realm, and Christ's authority works visibly and invisibly.

Case 19: A Long Distance Phone Deliverance

A pastor from north of my home had called me a month earlier, asking me to come and help a teenager in the church's youth group with extreme demonic problems. The staff was having difficulty in finalizing the deliverance. A friend of the pastor knew of my work in helping the demonized and gave him my name. It was a drive of several hours, but this would provide plenty of time to pray and sing to the LORD as I drove.

Upon arriving, the pastor shared details of previous prayer sessions. Ruth had been born into a family of generational witchcraft and had participated in it. Months earlier, she had received Christ as her Lord and Savior, and this is when the demons erupted in her. I stayed for less than a week to help the pastor with counseling and deliverance. She had a promiscuous background that would later reveal demonic entry. Driving home and praying, I thanked the LORD for His work in the girl's life. I was sad that Ruth's family offered her little support.

A few days after I got home, I received a call from Ruth. She was very depressed. We spent time talking about what her thought pattern was and how it induced the depression. Suddenly her voice changed, and I was listening to a seductive and flirtatious type of voice. It was clear that a demon had manifested, blocking Ruth out of the conversation.

Addressing the demon I said: "In the Name of Jesus, who are you?" The demon's response was "I am seduction." While seduction can be a lifestyle (sin of the flesh), it can also be a name just as "Hope," "Faith," "Precious," and "Joy" can be a name. Quickly the demon was cast out. This indwelling evil spirit had been trying to get Ruth back into sexual sin, but with Christ's help she resisted and called on the phone for counsel and prayer.

Teaching: When introduced to a new demonic situation, seek to find all areas of previous sinful participation. Help the person confess their sins, and ask the Lord Jesus to close the spiritual doors of previous demonic entry. With this knowledge, you can take authority over all demons that have entered through these sins and cast them out. Give encouragement and specific Scripture to the person to establish "faith that overcomes" (1 John 4:4; 5:4-5).

Case 20: The Pentagram Person Comes Back

A few years after we had tried to completely help the Texas lady who was initiated in the Pentagram, I moved back to my home town, about 50 miles from her. Joan did not know when or to where I had moved. For almost 15 years, we had no contact. No longer did I think of her any more. I had a family to take care of, and the LORD had pulled me out of counseling and casting out demons to focus on being a husband and father.

One Sunday morning, as we were preparing to go to church, my mother called me with astonishing information. There was a woman at her house named Joan who had driven an hour to see my mom. Joan had never met my mom, and my parents address had not been listed in the phonebook for over 20 years. Joan made it sound like she and I were friends, so my mother invited her in.

I told my mother I would be over immediately. As I drove to her house, less than a half mile away, I prayed for mom's protection and my family's protection from any demon activity that had *escorted* Joan to our town. This was another example of proving that demonic threats to follow me from many years ago were still active.

When I entered my mother's house, I discerned the same demonic presence that had been with Joan 15 years earlier. Joan was uneasy during our conversation which didn't last long. She could not explain how she got my mother's private address. During our conversation, she told me she had found a man to cast the demons out of her many years ago. When she told me his background, I knew she had gone to a man who used ritual exorcism without success, rather than trusting the Holy Spirit to supply the power for freedom. I asked her to leave and not come back. She never came back.

Teaching: Once you spend time directly involved in casting out demons and "they threaten to follow you" and cause problems, the evil spirits will wait for the opportune time to assault you, your family, or friends with various forms of oppression. They will even wait years in order to set you up or find the weak spiritual spot in your life. Some demonic attacks I have experienced include: evil spirits appearing in my house, bad dreams, constant irritability, intense headaches, difficulty sleeping, being slandered, blurry vision when trying to read my Bible, craving food when I wasn't hungry, and non-repentant demonic people I tried to help sending curses through evil spirits to harass me.

Case 21: Unicorns Everywhere in Her Room

After my college graduation, I lived in Fresno, California for 9 years. As I grew in my faith, Christian campus groups asked me to speak and present the Gospel. On one occasion, I spoke at a sorority house that was packed with over 75 people shoulder to shoulder. People sitting on the floor were within 10 feet of me.

The room was warm and near the end of the message a trickle of sweat ran down from behind my left ear to my collarbone. With the Bible in my left hand, I reached across my throat with my right index finger to wipe away the sweat. My message continued, and then it was time to ask if any wanted to receive Christ to have their sins forgiven. A few hands went up, and they prayed to receive Jesus as their Lord and Savior. Time was spent with those who made a decision to repent and receive Christ.

When the prayer time was over, a boy came up to me with a girl who came with him to hear the Gospel message. They introduced themselves, and Tina wanted to share what she saw happen to me toward the end of my message. This is how Tina described what she saw: "When you wiped the sweat from your throat area, your finger turned into a knife and started to cut your throat with blood coming out of the cut." I asked her if this was definitely what she saw, and she said "Yes." I told them I would like to continue this conversation in a place of privacy. They agreed.

We talked at her school dormitory in the entrance greeting area. I asked her various questions to see if she had previous or current occult involvement. As we talked, she told me of her interest in Mystical teachings. This made me think she might be involved in white witchcraft. I told her I would like to see her room and she agreed. The next day a Christian woman came with me, and we went to Tina's dorm room to search for any occult items.

As soon as we entered her room, we were shocked by the numerous unicorn posters and pictures she had all over her walls. Some of the posters had unusual colors around the unicorns to portray a spiritual-dimensional realm, not an earthly physical realm. Such visual ideas and beliefs are typically found in the New Age Mystical occult belief. Looking at the posters and pictures gave me the impression that the unicorn conveyed a captivating supernatural power connected to its beauty.

Unicorns are a controversial topic. Why? Because some believe they existed previously in a physical form on earth but are now extinct. Yet others believe in their ongoing existence in the spiritual realm with special powers. And some believe in both the physical and spiritual reality of unicorns.

The unicorn was depicted in ancient seals of the Indus Valley Civilization and was mentioned by the ancient Greeks in accounts of natural history by various writers, including Ctesias, Strabo, Pliny the Younger, and Aelian (Unicorn – Wikipedia).

The posters in Tina's room, with an eye-pleasing portrayal, pictured the unicorn as a horse with a horn on its forehead area above the eyes. The horn appeared to be 12-15 inches long, and the horn color varied from the color of the unicorn in the picture. Some pictures showed the horn in a spiral fashion. Small pictures of unicorns were also on the walls. Occult practitioners *believe* the horn has magical powers and can be used in unicorn imagery for healing spells, peace, comfort, inspiration, and love.

Tina was open to the fact that she had demonic problems and wanted help. She claimed to be a Christian. Tina admitted she believed the unicorn had some type of magical power. She would dwell upon the image of the unicorn. Before we pursued deliverance, we explained to her that unicorn power was not of the Holy Spirit. She accepted our counsel and agreed to tear down all the posters before we prayed for her. When the posters were removed and torn up, a time was set for her to meet us at an apartment. A school dormitory room is not a good place for casting out demons.

Lisa and I waited for her arrival. She came on time and was nervous, which is common for those seeking to have demon activity removed from their life. I explained that she might go unconscious or be aware (lucid) of when the demon manifested to resist the command to leave her. Tina sat on the carpet in a comfortable position. People should be given a choice to sit in a chair, on a couch, or on the floor, because demons can violently throw people to the floor when sitting at a table.

I looked at her and said, "In the Name of Jesus, I command the demon that made her see me cutting my throat during my Gospel presentation to come out of her!" She started squirming and shaking as the demon indwelling her manifested and began distorting her face. Tina was no longer a normal looking college student. The dark ugliness of the evil spirit was on her face and caused her to look very pale, as if she was sick. The evil spirit stared at us and resisted my command to leave her. She went semi-conscious and convulsed on the carpet.

This battle was short, because Tina had destroyed all her occult connections (pictures), and she was repentant for her sins. And the LORD was going to intervene in a powerful way with a verse He gave me to declare. It was Romans 1:4. I began saying repeatedly with authority to the demon: "According to Romans 1:4, the resurrection of Jesus from the dead declares with power that He is the Son of God. You must leave!" Within a minute, the demon exploded in rage and said:

"We know He is the Son of God! We never would have incited the people to kill Him if we had known He would come out of the tomb! Oh no!"

The demon realized he had admitted that the resurrection of Jesus declares Him to be God's Son, and he was startled by his confession by saying, "Oh No!" We began rejoicing in Christ's love, forgiveness, and resurrection power over all evil principalities and powers (Colossians 2:14-15). The Word of God, when used properly, is a weapon of our warfare for God's glory (Ephesians 6:17). The sword of the Holy Spirit drives out all fleshly evil and demons.

When the demon had left her, her face was calm. Closing prayer was given thanking Jesus for His power and love. Tina was relaxed, indicating no other demons still indwelled her. There were Bible-preaching churches near the University, so it was easy for her to get involved with a church for growth. It was comforting to know she had friends who attended a Bible preaching church.

Before closing this case, I need to address concerns about unicorns. If they existed at one time physically and are part of the LORD's creation, they *were not* created as evil animals. Genesis 1:31 teaches us that when God finished creation, "God saw everything that He had made, and, behold, it was very good." Demon-worshippers can take any animal Jesus created, such as an owl, and use it as an evil symbol of occult wisdom, but that does not mean all owls are evil.

However, if it can be proven that unicorns have never existed in physical form and exist only in the Mystical occult realm as spirit horses of supernatural power, then we should abstain and abhor any connection to them (1 Thessalonians 5:22). Stay away from any type of mythology unless researching to expose its evil. Remain consistent with true reality.

Teaching: Make sure the demonic person is sincerely repentant by having them openly confess their specific sins before the LORD in your presence. Also, check their residence thoroughly to see if all occult items have been surrendered and then destroyed (Acts 19:18-19). When a demon has revealed itself, as this one did at my Gospel message, upon meeting for deliverance, you can call it up and command it to leave. Have a friend make sure constant fellowship with quality Christians is part of their lifestyle. And make sure the delivered person is reading Christian literature and not wasting time on novels, which can cause mind-drifting, fantasy thoughts, and induce a type of imagery or creative visualization that invites demons back for oppression.

Case 22: Out of Her Body with Astral Projection

A good friend, who had watched his dad cast out demons at the church his dad pastored, called me with a request. He had met a woman who lived about an hour away from us. Their conversation revealed that she was dabbling in witchcraft and wanted help to get rid of the evil spirits that were tormenting her. Her witchcraft practices had begun to frighten her. She had progressed to "astral projection."

Astral projection is when a demon-indwelled person asks a specific demon to project their spirit/soul into the spiritual realm to experience euphoric pleasures and "spy" or see unusual things. It can be frightening. There is a silver cord, or what some call a silver-blue cord, that is attached to the body. It stays connected to the soul as it roams the spiritual realm.

Some Christians don't believe this cord exists, but this is common knowledge in witchcraft and found in their literature. In God's inspired Word, Solomon mentions this silver cord used for astral projection in Ecclesiastes 12:6. I talked to a former white witch of many years who became a Christian and did astral projection. She knows it is authentic.

Don called me and told me the details. We met for more discussion and called Lindsey to see if she was still sincere. A time was set to meet in her hometown and talk with her during the day. This would allow us to get complete information on her occult involvement and prepare with prayer. We could also remove and destroy any occult-connected items prior to commanding demons to leave her.

Lindsey asked us to meet in her apartment. When we arrived, we were greeted by a pale and frightened woman. She began to tell us about her occult life. Lindsey thought she had control of the spirits around her. But when she freely went into astral projection, the demon that functioned in this area was too strong for her to control. It would take her out of her body when she did not want to travel in the astral realm.

As her confession of occult involvement continued, suddenly we were faced with a decision. The indwelling demons were shaking her with fear. Her speech was sporadic. Do we begin casting them out now or set up a time later? Our answer came in a few seconds, because the demons increased their convulsions in her. This revealed that the Holy Spirit was uprooting them for removal. She asked for our help, so Don and I called upon the Lord Jesus for His power.

I began to cast out the demons that were causing the convulsions and slurring or stammering of her speech, as Don praised Jesus for His power. We saw demonic shadows of darkness with different shapes come out of her face and chest area. They left quickly. However, Lindsey knew the main demon that functioned in astral projection was still inside her. I commanded it to leave her in Jesus' Name, and Lindsey screamed as she saw it exit through her lower body. As it came out, it seemed to stretch and elongate during its departure.

The room had become still. No more demons were left to cast out. She asked God's forgiveness for her sins and gave her life to Christ as her Lord and Savior. This was the beginning of the LORD guiding her to a consistent relationship with Jesus and marrying a Christian man who understood her previous spiritual problem and supported her.

Less than 6 months before Lindsey was to marry, her husband called me. He said Lindsey was feeling an ongoing battle "on the inside" like she did when she had previous demonic problems. He asked me to come and pray for her. I said I would be there that night. When I saw her, she was uncontrollably restless and definitely needed prayer. The three of us prayed for Christ to help us.

Within 10 minutes of discussing her concerns, Lindsey began to undergo a visible pale countenance change. Shaking, "she fell to the floor." Before she passed out she said: "Don't let the demons that will be cast out go around any family members!" Commanding the demons to be cast out, I said what Lindsey had requested and the demons left. The evil spirits were gone in a few seconds. We spent time trying to figure out how demon activity had invaded Lindsey after she had been set free, but did not come to a specific answer.

They were married and enjoyed their Christian life for 7-10 years. Jesus blessed them with children. However, the demons waited for an opportune time to come back and deceive them. This couple always seemed to find something wrong with the church they were attending and kept bouncing around to find "the right church." Living without God's truth in the Santa Cruz-Aptos area, an area well-known for New Age Mystical practices and demon activity, led to their downfall.

Eventually they went to a very conservative church that didn't believe in the gifts of the Holy Spirit (1 Corinthians 12:1-11) and didn't believe Christians could have demonic problems like she had undergone. Lindsey and her husband had seen demons cast out of her. Yet eventually, they were convinced that Lindsey *never* had a demonic problem. I found out about their denial of demonic problems from their daughter more than 20 years after Jesus had set this "astral projection witch" free to serve Him. Instead, she succumbed to "wicked darts for denial" (Ephesians 6:16), self-induced delusion, and had chosen to live in a "dungeon of deception."

Their daughter also told me something that disappointed me and hurt. She said her mom was now convinced she was never demon-possessed, and I was demon-possessed when I helped her many years ago. Now this is a bit strange, because Lindsey no longer believed a Christian could have a demon in them, yet she had never questioned my salvation for many years. Did this mean she believed I was never a Christian? Even her in-laws had been told of her previous deliverances. However, Lindsey was determined to revise the story and resist the truth. To this day, she and her husband still believe a lie.

Teaching: When people get set free from demons in them, they must have fellowship with a congregation that has people who understand spiritual warfare. Otherwise, false teachings about demon activity can eventually enter their mind and heart and convince them to live a life of lies and denial of truth. The demons will plant false thoughts in so-called friends, pastors, and elders to transfer the deception to the once demon-indwelled person, eventually persuading them to believe they never had a demonic problem. This woman had multiple frightening demonic astral projection occurrences, yet over time demons convinced her to deny them.

Sometimes you can meet for discussion with a person with demons, not planning to cast out demons, but the Holy Spirit wants it done at that time. So always be ready to labor for Jesus in accordance to His will. Another thing a person can do to remind them of Christ's deliverance, love, and forgiveness is to put the date He set them free in a special place in their Bible. Then they will be reminded to thank Him often throughout their life. The LORD is always very good (Lamentations 3:22-23).

Case 23: Easter Sunday Choir Deliverance

When working with demonic people, I like to take them to church, if they will go, to let them see how pleasant Sunday mornings can be (Hebrews 10:24-25). Hearing the Word of God brings faith in Jesus (Romans 10:17).

Some demons had been cast out of a man I had been counseling, and he was interested in going with me to an Easter Sunday choir presentation at my home church. The place was packed. It was hard to find a seat. However, there was an empty spot in the padded bench to the left of Bill. As you will see, God had preplanned the need for that space.

The songs sung by the choir were fantastic. The sanctuary was filled with praise. Hands were lifted and faces wore smiles. At the end of one song, the music minister paused for a moment and asked a man to come to the center microphone for a solo. The song he sang was "O Happy Day." He sang it beautifully, and the people were stunned with silence so the words could penetrate their hearts.

When he got to the words "He washed my sins away," the demon in Bill turned his head to me and gave me a dirty look. Bill started shaking, and the demon came out of his mouth with a gush of air. Bill was knocked down to his left on the padded bench where that one special area was *not* occupied by a person. The lady seated to the left of Bill glanced at him, looked a little startled, ignored him, and then went back to listening to the song.

After the Easter special, Bill went to the pastor and shook his hand. Then he told the pastor that he had been delivered from a demon during the music. The pastor smiled and said "Good." Then the pastor looked at me and nodded his head, acknowledging that he knew I was working with this man. It was of great comfort to attend a church where the staff supported my gift in this area of reconciling people (2 Corinthians 5:19) to salvation in Jesus. Music has a powerful influence in people, as will be shown in the next two cases.

Teaching: Music that glorifies the LORD has the power to comfort, to heal, to strengthen, and in this case, to drive out a demon. The LORD's music has "the loving power" to make evil spirits depart (1 Samuel 16:23). At the opposite end of the music spectrum, where disruptive instrument beats (dissonance) and improper (sinful) words are voiced, music has the power to invite evil spirits into the presence of people, and in some cases into their bodies.

When one reads this case, it is obvious that God's plan was carried out perfectly during an Easter song, a song that honors the sin-cleansing blood of Jesus, God's only Savior (Acts 4:12). Thirty five years later Bill is still serving the Lord Jesus Christ, proving that Jesus "washed his sins away," and believing "There is power in the blood."

Case 24: A German Composer Named Wagner

Richard Wagner was born on May 22nd, 1813, and passed away on February 13th, 1883. He was one of Adolf Hitler's favorite composers. Why was Hitler fond of Wagner? History records that Wagner was against the Jews (anti-Semitic), and Hitler's Holocaust hatred of the Jews will always be a well-established historical fact.

My dad was a Medic in the Battle of the Bulge in Germany in World War II. He served in the 104th Infantry Division as a Timberwolf. The details of the Timberwolf success are recorded in *Timberwolf Tracks,* 1946 edition. My dad saw the death chambers, and said you could smell the horrible odor of death in the air all around them.

In case 2, I mentioned that Lindy had done research on the occult involvement of the Nazis in World War II. Her research had included finding information on Adolf Hitler and his special attraction to composer Richard Wagner. *Judaism in Music* (1850) "was the first of Wagner's writing to feature anti-Semitic views" (Richard Wagner –Wikipedia).

Wagner also argued "that Jewish musicians were only capable of producing music that was shallow and artificial, because they had no connection to the genuine spirit of the German people" (Wagner Controversies –Wikipedia). Did Wagner ever read or study the Psalms? They were written by Jews and are filled with the melody of beautiful music. The Psalms are not "shallow and artificial." They are deep with beauty, valuable teachings, praise to the LORD, *and* Holy Spirit genuine!

The purpose of the information on Richard Wagner is significant as will be shown. After Lindy was set free from Damien and other demons, she bought a Christian album of praise and soft music. While I was at her apartment with friends listening to her new album, something of great importance happened. During one song, the vocals stopped for about 30 seconds and instrumental choir music filled in, and then the vocals came back to finish the song. Lindy became uneasy.

She asked me to stop the music to check something on the long play record. I handed it to her, and she went to the 30 second section to see who the composer was. It was Richard Wagner. Immediately she told me to destroy the album. Lindy was not going to mix or share an hour of the LORD's music in a 30 second spot with a person connected to Hitler's demonic mass murder regime.

Lindy's sensitivity to a few seconds of an evil composer intertwined with beautiful Christian music is *a needed example* of discernment that all Christians should exercise. A little leaven (Galatians 5:9) opens the door for ongoing deception, and evil will find a home for wicked growth. What is sad is that Christian musicians continue to mix a demonic rock beat with

103

Christian lyrics and think it is okay with God. Demons like rock music that improperly motivates the body and emotions and does not give the inner spirit a calm to be sensitive to continuous Holy Spirit guidance.

Are there any music CDs you need to destroy, because they are destroying part of your relationship with Jesus? Do you need to quit listening to so-called Christian radio stations that play songs the Lord Jesus would not listen to or sing? Don't remain in sin. Do what is right for God's glory (James 4:17).Even Christian music can have a demonic insertion in the words or rhythm.

Teaching: After people are set free from demon activity, spend time with them discussing what music and literature they are considering for purchase. Bookstores are filled with New Age books, Mystical beliefs, strange ways to pray to God that are not found in Scripture (mantras, prayer centering, circle drawn prayers), and many books by authors who promote that it is God's will to heal and prosper all "by faith." The "Health and Wealth gospel" belief is an entirely different gospel. My book titled, *Are Word of Faith Televangelists Misleading Millions* explains the deception that "The Threefold Gospel of Redemption" portrays.

Also, do not be surprised if a person you helped with demonic problems points out an area where you need help to be more effective in your calling. Such correction usually comes after an ongoing friendship is in progress, not immediately after the final deliverance session.

Case 25: Confronting Orpheus, a Musical Demon

Helping demonic people does not always require that when you visit the afflicted it will be a time of casting out evil spirits. Establishing a trusting friendship and respect for your counsel is vital so that their trust is in Christ working through you.

I had been working with a man who had a family line of practicing witchcraft for over 200 years, but he wanted out of it to become a Christian. William and I became friends as soon as we met and spent time talking about the Bible. He had questions about specific things in the Bible. With

104

friends, answers were provided that he accepted as God's truth. It was a God-ordained friendship that exists to this day. I will always admire William for his devotion as a father, husband, teacher, and seeker of truth to glorify the LORD.

It was one of those nights when I went to visit a friend with demonic problems, but had not planned to battle demons. Fellowship and some munchies were in my mind, as well as anything he wanted to discuss. The conversation drifted to his music choices. He was blessed with plenty of musical talent. He taught music in school and gave private lessons.

Within a few minutes, a demon spoke through William and said, "I am Orpheus, the god of music." I commanded Orpheus to be quiet, and I began to ask William about all his studies in music. He said he had studied Greek Mythology, knew of the Orpheus influence in music, and studied Brazilian Flamenco music. As the discussion continued, he admitted the famous Flamenco guitarist he studied and patterned some of his music after had an occult background. It was during this time of discussion that the room atmosphere began to become unpleasant.

Flamenco music can vary in cultures. Typically it is a type of music with an upbeat tempo (the guitar often plays a disruptive beat) that encourages both jerky and smooth body movement, fast foot tapping, quick hand clapping, spinning, and is accompanied with a seductive look when done by an individual. Flamenco dancers also dance in a line. If you watch Flamenco dance on You Tube, it is obvious the movements are to stimulate the fleshly desires and sensuality.

The guitar William had purchased was expensive, and he used it for the Flamenco style of music. When he was sure of his sin of using the guitar to play evil music, he said he would destroy the guitar if that is what God wanted. I told him the guitar was not evil and did not need to be destroyed. He dedicated his guitar to Jesus and to never play Flamenco music again. Then he destroyed his Flamenco sheet music.

Now it was time to cast out Orpheus and any demons connected to William's music. With a command to "Leave in Jesus' Name," Orpheus

105

and any other demons with an occult music connection were gone without a verbal fight and only a slight physical show of resistance. William's repentance and submission to counsel from the Word of God broke the power of the demonic stronghold.

Teaching: Any time you visit a person you have counseled, and you know they still have demonic issues, you must be clean of all sins and be ready to serve Jesus. From what I have learned, there are two reasons why demons usually manifest through a person when I visit them: (1) It is time for them to be removed from the person's life. (2) They are trying to get you to waste your time talking to them, which is a form of Spiritism.

Music is a powerful form of spiritual and physical persuasion. Satan and his demons know this. They have had thousands of years to study how music can influence people to sin and control them. We need to be very careful with the type of music we allow into our life. Our selection should always be music that Jesus would listen to while sitting beside us.

Decades have passed since William renounced Brazilian Flamenco music and dedicated his guitar to Jesus. He still plays music to please his Lord Jesus. Take time to see if there is any music style in your life that is offensive to Jesus. If found, ask Him to replace it with words and a rhythm that He would like to hear in your life.

Case 26: A Demon Cast Out in a Hospital

As I picked up the phone, I could tell this person was desperate for help. His mother was in a hospital and dying. When she was first admitted, she could no longer eat anything. Now she was having trouble drinking water. John asked me if a death curse could be put on a person. I told him "Yes, if the person knew exactly how to summon a specific demon for this function." This was an urgent matter and needed prayer quickly.

A time was set to meet that day. John told me about a very wicked woman who hated his mother, and told his mother she would "put a death curse on her." He asked me again if it was possible for a witch to do this. I said it was possible. Missionaries have told of death curses (Voodoo

106

witchcraft) that came to pass on their mission field. I know of people who have visited Haiti, and it has a history of death curses.

We got up and went to the hospital. I met his mother, and she looked so pale and sick. An IV tube was in her arm to give her fluids, yet her vital signs continued to weaken. Beatrice told me about the evil lady and how her current sickness had begun shortly after the witch had said she would activate the death curse.

John and I decided to pray for her and something stood out quickly. After about 10-15 seconds of prayer, her face became contorted. She looked masculine, began to spit, and a voice in another tongue began to speak out of her. They were Portuguese, and I asked John if he understood those words. He said "No. I've never heard my mother speak that language." I told him she had demon in her, and it needed to be cast out to break the death curse. Beatrice remembered nothing.

We were in a Catholic hospital and went to the people in charge. She was in a semi-private room. The situation was explained to them about needing to cast out a demon. They knew this woman was dying and granted our request to have the other person out of the room by 9 am the next morning. John called his siblings and told them what had happened at the hospital. They were believers in Christ and wanted to be with us at the hospital in prayer the next day.

Prayers continued that night, asking for the death curse to be removed. We met at 9 am the next morning at the hospital, gathered around the bed, and began to ask the LORD to drive out the demon. Within a few seconds, the demon came up spitting at us and speaking in an ugly language. All the children began to tell the demon to leave their mother "In the Name of Jesus," and in less than a minute it was gone.

A noticeable facial coloring began to appear on Beatrice. She smiled and began to talk to us. Then she asked for some water and drank it. We told the nurses that she was drinking water, and they brought her some juice. She drank a little. Later at lunch time, she ate food for the first time in days. After she ate dinner, she had the strength to walk. Her vital signs were checked, and she was released to go home that same day. The family had an evening of holy celebration.

It should be noted that I did not want to argue with John about whether his mother was saved or not saved prior to the deliverance. When the demon was cast out, Beatrice prayed to dedicate her life to Christ and follow Him. Personally, I don't believe a physical death curse will come to pass on a Christian, but I remain open to correction. Weeks later, it was good to hear Beatrice was doing well and maintaining her health.

I have a friend who has traveled the world for over 30 years and done hundreds of deliverances. One evening while he was in Hawaii, he was preparing to see a public Kahuna ceremony for understanding the cultural mindset of the Hawaiians. He got up to go to it but was suddenly weak, became sick, and had to go to bed. He told me he had not prayed for protection (no armor) before he started to attend the ceremony. Perhaps demons can make Christians sick if they go into Satan's territory (apart from God's will) without praying for protection from all demon activity.

Teaching: When going to a hospital to see a demonized person, pray for God to prepare the minds of the staff to accommodate the person's needs. Make sure all who participate in the prayer session for deliverance are Christians. Also, pray for God to protect and shield the prayer team from all demon activity. Hospitals can have demon activity from floor to floor if medical treatment is mixed with New Age beliefs.

Case 27: Christ's Power Frightened Him

While I was a contracted carpet cleaner, every four months for two weeks, I drove to San Diego to spend time cleaning carpet and tile in stores in that county. The gym in Solana Beach was one of my favorite places to work out. The beach was fun and the basketball court was constantly occupied with players. My first cleaning stop was in El Cajon.

Entering the store, I introduced myself to Gary, the manager. We got into conversation quickly. He was into body surfing, and we talked about the thrill of doing it. During our conversation, I noticed that Gary was quite nervous as time passed. I told him I'd be back a half hour before closing to bring my cleaning equipment inside.

Later as I cleaned the carpets and tile, we talked more. When I was finished, it was late, and we were both hungry. Our choice was a Denny's restaurant. We ordered our food, and eventually Gary told me: "You had the most power of anyone who had ever walked into this store, and it scared me." Hundreds of people had come through the front door of his store. Jesus doesn't entertain people with His healing and deliverance power. This told me Gary had a definite need and Jesus wanted to help him.

I was able to sway the conversation to discussing Jesus. Gary began to get unusually nervous as we talked more about Jesus. Slightly shaking, he began withdrawing to the back of the booth and didn't want to look at my eyes. We decided we would go to his apartment and finish our talk. Following him, I prayed for wisdom, discernment, and for Gary to receive Jesus as his Lord and Savior. From previous demonic encounters, I knew the invisible spiritual battle was already taking place.

As we entered his apartment, Mike, his roommate, greeted us. The three of us sat at the kitchen table and talked about Jesus. Suddenly Gary became sort of dizzy. I reached to his hand on the table to comfort him and heard a deep voice come out of his mouth saying: "Don't touch him." I looked at Mike and asked him if this was frightening. Mike's response was "No, because I had demons cast out of me before I became a Christian."

When you know there is a demon inside a person in a setting like this, you can rebuke it and command it to leave. Or you can pray to the LORD to see if He wants to make the demon reveal how it entered the person. When the sin of entry is known *and confessed*, the evil spirit has no right to stay in the person and will be cast out. We waited less than a minute and the demon, by the power of the Holy Spirit, was forced to tell how Gary opened the door for demonic entry.

The evil spirit said "Gary's constant hatred for his father provided my opening." I commanded the demon to be muzzled and not interfere with me as I talked to Gary. When Gary came out of his unconscious state, I

109

asked Gary about his hatred for his father. He looked at me and said, "How did you find out? I have never told anyone how much I hated my dad."

Gary's dad had suffered a disabling injury a few years earlier, and Gary was given sole responsibility to care daily for his father. He began to hate the responsibility and then transferred his hatred to his dad. Finally he was able to leave his dad's home, but his hatred for his father didn't leave him, nor did the demonic spirit that had entered him. Though Mike confirmed everything to Gary the demon said about the hatred issue, Gary didn't want the demon cast out, did not want to confess his sin of hatred, nor did he want to receive Jesus to have his sins forgiven. He just stared.

This stunned me. Now I knew why the LORD didn't want me to cast out the demon. Gary didn't care about surrendering his life to Jesus or having the demon cast out. No amount of talking from me or his roommate could persuade Gary to trust Jesus. He was determined to lead his own life.

Occasionally, during the next three years, I would see Gary at the El Cajon store, and he still had no desire to receive Jesus as his Lord, nor have the demon cast out. This one hurt me for years. I still pray for Gary.

Teaching: Sometimes the LORD makes it clear that a person is indwelled with a demon, but the person doesn't care. Is it possible that demons can sear a conscience to desensitize a person so it doesn't make sense to get rid of the demon? Is it possible Gary wanted to retain his hatred for his father and didn't care if a demon was involved with enhancing the hatred? Was Gary afraid he would have to apologize to his father and care for him again?

This is an example of why we don't immediately command a demon to leave a non-repentant person, because the demon may leave from indwelling but come back later with more vengeance upon realizing the person has no restriction power of the Holy Spirit (Luke 11:24-26).

Case 28: Lack of Peace and a Sick Baby

While receiving my education at Fresno State University, I met some wonderful people in my classes. A Christian named Randy and I developed a friendship. We talked about various Bible topics, and eventually we discussed how demon activity is evident in Scripture. Randy seemed to have an interest in the topic of spiritual warfare.

During one of our discussions, I mentioned that I had seen demons cast out of people. Randy looked at me and began to ask questions about how demons enter people. When I told him occult participation and occult books can invite demons into a person's presence, he looked at me in a perplexed manner. He asked some questions, and then told me he had previously purchased an occult book out of curiosity. He also mentioned that their baby had been sick and the peaceful atmosphere in their house was no longer consistent

He wanted me to come to his place and pray. The next day I went and met his wife. Rita was a pleasant person, devoted to serving her husband and a loving mother. No spiritual division had occurred between them, but both agreed the peaceful presence they had enjoyed was no longer in their house. As we talked, I sensed that a "different presence" could be felt in the room. That presence was between Randy and me.

With my numerous past exposures to demonic activity in or around a person, I knew now was time to get to the root of the problem. I asked Randy to get the occult book he had purchased and hand it to me. He reached up on his bookshelf to get it. As he turned to give it to me, an evil looking face was in front of his face glaring at me. Randy was suddenly nervous. As soon as he gave the book to me, he became relaxed. The book was taken outside and destroyed.

Randy confessed his sin of purchasing and bringing a "cursed object of abomination" (Deuteronomy 7:26; Acts 19:18-20) into his house. That night the peace of Jesus was restored, but there was a concern. Their little baby had been sick with a fever and medicine had not eliminated it. Rita knew what to do. Throughout the night, she prayed for her baby, praised the LORD often, and carried her at times when she cried. This went on for hours, until sunrise. Suddenly they were greeted with a beautiful sunrise and a daughter whose fever was gone. This event changed their life.

Eventually, Randy and Rita went to the mission field. Beautiful Christian people.

Teaching: Any book or object that has a link to the occult, where demons dwell, should never be purchased and must be destroyed when removed from a person's residence. There is no proof that every purchase of an occult-linked item will bring a demon into your residence. However, when you know something is evil you should not become involved with it. The father is the head of the house and is primarily responsible for the spiritual covering and protection of all who live with him.

Because of *when* the forbidden book was brought into their house, and the onset of their child's illness and resistance to medicine, they believed this sin delayed their daughter's quick recovery. That is between them and the LORD. One thing they knew; reading the Bible would always show them what God wanted them to know about any topic.

Case 29: His Picture Was a Spell

A Christian college student named Danielle gave me a call on a pleasant, quiet, and warm afternoon. She asked if I helped people with demonic problems. I told her I did. Then she began to provide some details on a relationship she wanted to end, but was struggling to end it. She sounded very troubled and asked to come see me.

Within ten minutes, she arrived. Sitting at the kitchen table, she asked if a Christian could be influenced by a spell from another person. I said it was possible if the Christian was living in sin. She had been dating a man who was not a Christian, and after a few months Danielle realized he was not interested in Jesus. When she tried to break it off completely, he told her it wasn't going to happen, because he would make sure she continued to think of him. His confident statement caused ongoing concern.

As we continued our discussion, Danielle said her bedroom had become a place of uneasiness. I asked her if she had any jewelry or clothing from the man. She didn't, but suddenly she remembered she had a picture of him on her dresser. And now the Holy Spirit reminded her that he said he would "put a spell on his picture so she would think of him." She gasped as she told me that there was something about his picture that lured her to look at it. Trembling, she told me she had wanted to throw out the picture but never got around to doing it.

Danielle now knew she had sinned by dating an unbeliever who had been using witchcraft on her to control the relationship. He had sent an evil spirit to her room to remind her of him when she looked at his picture. She said his picture would be destroyed when she went back to her apartment.

With her body slightly shaking and her voice occasionally stuttering, she began to ask the LORD to forgive her sin. By the end of her prayer, she was calm and portrayed a relaxed countenance. Immediately the picture was destroyed, and never did Danielle sense an uneasy or evil presence in her room.

She went right back to a Gospel preaching church, phoned to let me know things were going well with Jesus, and six months later she was engaged to a Christian man of God.

Teaching: If a Christian gets into a sinful relationship with someone who knows witchcraft spells, then a spell could be put on the Christian. Only through repentance and destruction of all objects obtained during the spiritual and or physical immoral relationship will deliverance be granted. Christians need to obey 2 Corinthians 6:14-18. Before dating a person, get some spiritual history on the person and a personal testimony of when a commitment was made to repent and follow Jesus. Go to some church functions together, and spend time reading the Bible together.

As previously mentioned, objects can be used by occult people who know how to call upon demons to spend time around that specific object to manipulate the intended person. In this case, it was a picture. Demons do not need to inhabit an object to accomplish a curse or spell.

Case 30: Her Pretty Anklet Was Evil

A friend called me and asked if he and another friend could bring a Christian girl over to talk with me about a spiritual problem. My heart and apartment were always open for fellowship, prayer, and whatever the LORD had for us to do.

The three of them arrived later that day. After introductions, I listened to Jenny share what had been troubling her. She had not been sleeping well and had sensed an unpleasant presence around her, one she had never experienced. She was active in her relationship with Jesus, and there was no evidence that she was living a life of sin.

Jenny had not been involved with the occult "knowingly," but the Lord Jesus would soon expose *her* "unknown" occult involvement. The minutes went by as we asked for Christ's help, and Jenny remained stressed and emotionally uneasy. I lowered my head to silently seek the LORD. As I looked at the carpet, I noticed she had an anklet on her left ankle with various items attached to it.

Looking up at Jenny, I asked her about the anklet and the items on it. With a surprised look, she said she had "forgotten" about this gift given to her recently by a female classmate. At a university campus, it is easy to develop friendships with classmates for exam study. These study times feature food, coffee, and sometimes a gift exchange as friendships deepen through people spending more time together.

When we looked at the anklet, we recognized one "occult charm" accompanied by several other pieces of beauty hanging on the chain. Jenny was not sure if the person who gave her this anklet knew exactly what that charm meant. But it definitely had agitated Jenny's personal relationship with Jesus. Jenny asked us to destroy it (break it) and throw it in the trash, and we did. His peace came back to her. We prayed and she went away with relief and a smile.

Teaching: Through ignorance, people purchase items and sometimes have no idea that they have an occult connection. Jenny's case does not mean that every time a chain or anklet has an occult item attached to it that a demon will automatically follow the purchased item. But demons can watch from the spiritual realm, and if they see their items as spiritual contact points, they can follow the owner of the item of sin (Deuteronomy

114

7:26; Acts 19:18-19). Choose jewelry items that glorify the Lord and stir up conversation to share the Gospel.

This is an example of a person "unknowingly" wearing an occult charm on her body, and it disrupted the peace in her spiritual life. Christians must remember that their bodies are "the temple of the living God" (2 Corinthians 6:16-17), and He doesn't like demonic items attached to His redeemed people. Be wise when you purchase any gift of jewelry. Some of the turquoise stones used in Native American cultures have a direct link to the evil spirit realm, as do "Dream catchers."

Also, the discount jewelry stores have items that are fashioned out of direct recognition to ancient gods, such as crystals and "energy stones." Jesus did not teach His followers to use physical objects as a spiritual way to contact His heavenly Father. He taught us to pray, ask, call upon, or to talk to God personally about our needs and the needs of other people.

I am often disappointed when I visit a Christian's house and see worldly, garbage books on their shelves that have no spiritual value for growth in Jesus as Lord and Savior. Christians sin by not making the most of their time (Ephesians 5:15-17). They waste time by reading fantasy novels or a witchcraft series such as the Harry Potter books. Jesus wouldn't read Harry Potter books. He would burn them. Do you need to burn some fantasy witchcraft literature that stimulates your mind to worthless and vain imaginations? (2 Corinthians 10:5).

Are you raising your children with literature that will stimulate their curiosity to "check out" witchcraft that could bring demon activity in their lives and yours? And is sin being stored on your cell phones?

Case 31: Is Incubus a Real Sexual Demon?

This question has stirred up significant controversy among Christians. Why? Occult practitioners with vast knowledge will testify that Incubus is a literal demon involved with providing sexual satisfaction to women who want it. They also will adamantly state that "Succubus" is a demon who will provide sexual satisfaction to men. However, Christians ignorant of what demons can do will say, "There is no way a specific sexual demon can be involved in a person to enhance their sexual satisfaction." The following information will shed light on this debated topic.

I had been spending time sharing Jesus with a witch. While talking to Isabel one night, the subject of demon activity among witches transpired. The topic of a sex demon named "Incubus" was part of the conversation. She explained rituals and said they could be used to contact demons for various reasons, and the demon named "Incubus" was available for sexual satisfaction.

Suddenly her eyes and her face changed, and I could discern that a demon was taking over her personality. I said "In the Name of Jesus, Who are you?" Here is the demon's response: "You know who I am. You were talking about me. I am Incubus." Immediately I commanded Incubus to "Leave in Jesus' Name!" He was gone in seconds.

The witch admitted she had conjured up Incubus to enter her to enhance sexual satisfaction. She was embarrassed but felt some relief. Now here is the good news. This lady became a Christian and treated me like a son she never had.

Teaching: When discussing Jesus with someone you know who has occult involvement, be prepared for the unexpected. Always pray for Christ's wisdom, protection, and for Jesus to remove the blinding power upon their minds placed by Satan to keep them from the Gospel (2 Corinthians 4:4). People coming out of the occult need to immediately start reading the Bible and develop a consistent praise and prayer life. Having them memorize Philippians 4:4-9 is essential. Check on them often, and get them involved with a Bible study and a home church. They have much insight to offer us in our spiritual growth.

Case 32: He Did a Midnight Crossroads Ritual

A close friend of mine had a difficult childhood. He was adopted by a Mormon family that showed favoritism toward their older biological son. Wesley did not believe in Mormonism teachings that contradicted the

116

Bible. He knew the Jesus of the Bible was the only way to have his sins forgiven.

He was an exceptional football player in high school and college. While playing community college football, he received letters of interest from the Kansas City Chiefs, the Dallas Cowboys, and the Oakland Raiders. But one day he received a letter he did not like. It was from the draft board, and he was required to report for duty to serve in Vietnam. Wesley signed up and wanted to be a paratrooper. He finished his training in Georgia and rotated with 120 paratroopers to Vietnam. After a year of duty, only 20 were alive. He spent time with prostitutes in opium dens to cover the pain of what he saw and had to do. The horrors of war took a heavy toll on his mind, and he was released with a medical discharge.

Back in the states, he wandered around from job to job. He became an alcoholic, was set free from addiction, then became a heroin addict, and struggled with relapses much of his life. He also became involved with the occult in his thirties, a curiosity that had carried over from Vietnam.

A Christian lady knew Wesley and I were friends. She had recently seen him and was worried about his curiosity with witchcraft. A time for the three of us to get together for conversation was set. It was good to see Wesley again, but he seemed to have no peace and had trouble relaxing while we talked.

As time passed, we got to the heart of his problem. He was much deeper in the occult than basic curiosity. Wesley mentioned that he had done a specific blood ritual to conjure up a demon one time. What he did shocked us. He said he got a chicken, went to a country crossroad, cut off the chicken's head at midnight, poured the blood on the center of the crossroad, and said specific words to conjure up a demon.

Quickly, and to his unprepared surprise, a large, vicious-looking demon appeared by the blood. Wesley was frightened, ran back to his car and left the scene. He was trembling more and more as he told this story. We knew he was indwelled with a demon, perhaps more than one. He wanted help from the demonic turmoil he went through daily, so a date was set up in my apartment. He prepared with prayer, and was ready to give his life to Jesus.

We prayed, and when the time came we were thankful for God's protection. Wesley sat in a recliner and quickly began shaking as we started praying. A demon was commanded to leave him and almost threw him out of the chair. It left, but what was left behind was sickening. When the demon came out of him, it left a foul odor that filled the room. It smelled like a combination of manure and sulfur. In all my deliverance experience, a demon had never left behind such a filthy odor in the air.

It took about a minute for the air to clear. Then we went back to commanding other demons to leave Wesley, but the Devil had more distractions planned. My attention turned to the front door. A demonic spirit about six feet tall walked through the door. Its head was shaped like a huge fly. Others saw it, too. We rebuked it and commanded it to leave. It disappeared, but to our left more smaller demons began to pass through the west wall. We commanded them all to leave and asked the LORD to put a stop to it. God answered our prayer. No more demons entered.

However, that seemed to be all the LORD was going to do that night. We ended in prayer and Wesley went home. We had another prayer session at a country house, but there was no finality. I explained to the Christian lady that I might not be the one Jesus wanted to use in completing the deliverance. She began calling friends and found a Christian counseling office about three hours away. Their counseling was done from the Bible, and they had helped demonized people come out of the occult into a saving relationship with Jesus.

Wesley spent time with them and they finished what I couldn't. They encountered a strong demon named Mephistopheles, and when he was cast out freedom was evident. Wesley repented, renounced all his witchcraft sins and committed his life to following Jesus. Though the demons had been cast out, Wesley would need years of inner healing from his Vietnam exposure, his choice of doing drugs, his rejection as an adopted son, and the spiritual turmoil caused by various demons that had indwelled him.

Teaching: Sometimes Jesus uses people only in the beginning to lay a foundation for freedom in deliverance. It became evident as I spent time with Wesley that another person or group would be selected by Jesus to end the demonic occupation inside Wesley's body. I was not jealous that someone else did what I could not do, because the victory is in Christ's authority, which He grants according to His will. Also, when a person does any kind of a ritual to call up a demon, there will be an intense battle. My main mistake was not fasting and praying enough before beginning to pray for him, and I should have asked the others who helped to fast with me.

Case 33: Lord Jesus Sends Me to the Desert

Within a year after I was saved, I developed an interest in sound doctrine. I wanted to know the main doctrine the early Body of Christ was taught, and how to defend the true faith (Jude 3). Upon learning the important doctrines that were essential to verify whether a person was a Christian, my learning was put to use. This led me to numerous encounters with Mormons, Jehovah's Witnesses, and The Way International. My interest in confronting the cults that knocked on doors grew.

A friend suggested I get in touch with an apologetic ministry in Los Angeles for more training. I did, and was blessed with men and women who helped me defend the true faith. During this time, the Lord Jesus had already used me to help the people cited in cases 1 and 2. I talked to the head man of the ministry and we connected. He knew God had called me to help people with demonic problems.

The apologetic ministry received a call from a man in the desert area of Banning, California. Matt had grown up in a family where occultism had been accepted. His mother had received a miraculous healing of her deformed foot (a birth defect) when she was young. She had always wanted to be a ballet dancer. The healing was good enough to last her for many years of travel to show her ballet talent.

Matt was a talented man. He had worked for Walt Disney in artistic animation, did a book cover for a worldwide best-selling Christian author, and made his gifts and talents available to many. He had recently become a Christian, but was plagued with depression and lack of satisfaction in his relationship with Jesus. He knew something was wrong inside of him, so he called the ministry in Los Angeles for help. They gave him Scriptures to read, suggested more prayer, but did not check his background to see if occult influence could be a factor.

This didn't remedy Matt's oppression, so he called them again to see if they could send someone to his area to help him. During this time, I had planned to visit the ministry in Los Angeles, so God's plan was falling into place. I received a call from them to see if I would drive to the desert to meet with this man. I said "Yes." For me, driving was fun, because I could pray, praise the LORD, sing, and listen to Christian music. Before I drove to see Matt, I called him. We had a great conversation. It was like I had already known him. The plan was for me to spend two days with him.

When I arrived in the afternoon, he greeted me with a big smile. We went inside to learn more about each other as friends before the questions and counseling would begin. Matt lived alone. I listened as Matt gave details about what made him think and believe he was indwelled with a demon. I told him that whenever I noticed a definite change in his countenance or vocal tone, we would discuss in detail the topic that had caused this change. He agreed.

After a light dinner, the LORD began to give me discernment to see when a demon would slightly change Matt's verbal tone. As the demonic change became more obvious during our conversation, I brought it to his attention. He agreed that there was a slight change when I mentioned it to him. He began to get excited, because previous people he talked to or asked for help never noticed this change.

More evidence of a demon talking through him continued, but only for a few words at a time. Now Matt realized when the indwelling demon would slip in a few words occasionally. I told him we were close to praying for his freedom. Then something very unusual came to my mind. I asked Matt if I could take a bath, not a shower, before we started our prayers. I prefer showers, but a bath was put on my mind. And the bath had a unique purpose.

While I was relaxing in the tub, Matt was in repentance as he sat on his bed. I don't have a voice that would sell in the music industry, but enjoy singing. As I began to sing quietly to myself, my voice got much stronger, sounded better, and echoed continually in the bathroom. Suddenly I began to sing these words loudly from the refrain in the song titled *Victory in Jesus*:

> O victory in Jesus, my Savior, forever. He sought me
> and He bought me with His redeeming blood; He loved
> me ere I knew Him, and all my love is due Him, He
> plunged me to victory, beneath the cleansing flood.

I did not know that a most unusual, Holy Spirit deliverance happened in the bedroom when I was singing. After toweling off and getting dressed, I was ready to pray and command all the demon activity to leave Matt. When I entered Matt's room, he had a big, relaxed smile on his face. This is what Matt told me.

> "When you started singing, the demon began to
> tremble inside me. When you got louder and sang
> about Christ's redeeming blood, the only demon left
> came out of my chest and ran out the wall."

We both thanked our Lord Jesus for His way, which was truly amazing. Matt had his freedom. Sleep that night was peaceful for both of us, and we needed it.

The next day Matt fixed breakfast and we spent time in fellowship. Before noon, I drove back to the ministry office in Los Angeles that had asked me to help Matt. No longer did Matt call for help. He knew how to call upon Jesus and pray for His protection.

Teaching: How the final demon was cast out of Matt is truly amazing. It shows that Jesus does deliverance and sets the captives free in His way. My role was to counsel Matt for understanding the needed repentance, and I was to obey by taking a bath instead of a shower. If you are wondering why Jesus had me take a bath rather than a shower, here is your answer: A shower is noisy when the water is running. Thus, my voice might not have been heard singing about Christ's blood in Matt's bedroom. But with a bath tub full, it would echo and go through the walls for God's glory. When called by the Lord Jesus to do the works of the Holy Spirit, you must be sensitive and aware of whatever comes to your mind.

Case 34: Demons Like the Doctrine of "Calvinism"

A pastor had asked for me to assist in a demonic case in his Baptist church. We had cast a demon out of a member of his youth group, but we knew more were left inside because the high school student was face down and unconscious at the office conference table. Slowly a demon manifested, made the person sit-up, and began to look around the room. It looked at me, then it looked at a pastor and fixed its haughty glare on him.

What this demon said should be been heard around the world by Christians who call themselves "Calvinists." If you want a complete understanding about this questionable doctrine concerning Christ's limited atonement and misrepresentation of His blood, you can look it up online. For the five point Calvinist, point number two is called "unconditional election." To them, this means from eternity God has *selected, elected, chosen, or predestined* some for Heaven *and* some for Hell, and it doesn't matter what man says. Therefore, all do not have the choice of going to Heaven. Thus, some were born *only* for the purpose of going to hell for eternity.

A close look at several easy to understand verses will confirm that "unconditional election," also known as *no* free choice for salvation, is not backed by the proper context of Scripture. Most scholars are convinced John wrote his Gospel and epistles *after* the other Gospels. A close look at

John's writings about Christ shows Jesus was not a Calvinist. Paul and Peter also penned wisdom on how Jesus wants us to understand "His atonement for all." With this in mind, we can see the accurate, clear context of what the apostles taught on "unconditional election" and "limited atonement."

> John 1:12 teaches "But *as many* as received Him, to them gave He power to become the sons of God, even to them that believe on His name."
>
> John 3:16 says "For God so loved the world (all humanity) that He gave His only begotten Son that *whosoever* believes in Him will have everlasting/eternal life."
>
> Romans 10:13 states that "*whosoever* shall call upon the name of the LORD shall be saved."
>
> 1 Timothy 4:10 directs us to "trust in the living God, who is the Saviour of *all* men..."
>
> 2 Peter 3:9 reveals that God is "not willing that any should perish, but that *all* should come to repentance."
>
> 1 John 4:14 declares that the *testimony* of the first century Christians who knew the truth is; "that the Father *sent* the Son to be the Saviour of the world."

Look back at the italicized words in these verses, and you will see and *know* that the Scriptures do not teach "Calvinism's unconditional election and limited atonement." Jesus never taught this false doctrine about His atonement, so the God-inspired writers of the New Testament didn't either.

However for generations, many have been misled by teachers who have misinterpreted some verses on predestination and have chosen to reject the repetitive clarity of the verses just presented. They believe and teach this false atonement doctrine that dishonors the cleansing blood of Jesus. His blood is *for as many* who repent of their sins. This helps demons in their quest to spread "doctrines of demons" and makes some believe they were predestined for Hell, with no chance for God's forgiveness. This is a horrible teaching.

This is what that repulsive demon said in a most taunting tone to the pastor who believed in the doctrine of Calvinism:

"Yeah, we really like it when people believe and teach that
God created some to go to heaven and some to go to hell.
It makes our work a lot easier! Haaaa, ha, ha, haaa!"

Immediately the demon went back down inside the person. The laugh was so shrilling. I asked the pastor if that was his belief. He said it was, and that was the way he was taught when getting his Bible degree. No more demons were cast out that day. We could only pray and counsel. The demon's taunting comment on Calvinism was a lesson to us on how demons are aware of false doctrine believed among Christians.

I came back at a later date to help the pastor finalize this deliverance. Before we started our prayer time, he told me he had reviewed the teaching that "some were created for Heaven and some were created for Hell." He had repented of his former belief. Eventually the person was set free.

Teaching: What this demon said to a specific Christian shows that demons have more awareness of false beliefs among Christians than we realize. This pastor had never said a word to me about his *false* Calvinist salvation belief, but at some point the demon found out and waited to use it against him. In another situation, I heard a demon brag out of a person about how he used a Christian to irritate a person undergoing demonic counseling. We took notes, approached the person operating in sin with our notes, and he repented. Congregational irritants should be brought to repentance (Matthew 18:15-17).

The pastor realized the demon knew of his sin of false doctrine and was convinced he must renounce it, or the Lord Jesus would not use him to help this person. You might question why the LORD would use a demon to expose a Christian's sin of false doctrine. God knows why in every situation (Romans 11:33-36) and does as He pleases (Psalm 115:3; Daniel 4:35).

Case 35: Eating Ice Cream and the Demon Leaves

It was a night when I just wanted to visit Brad, a demonized man I had been helping. My intent was not to confront any demons but to encourage him and discuss the Bible. After an hour, a demon took over his personality and began to speak through him, so I commanded it to leave. It would not exit the man and this perplexed me, because I had no desire to do deliverance when I visited the man. I began to wonder why the LORD allowed this demon to manifest.

I commanded the demon to leave him but it would not. I became quiet to see if the Holy Spirit might impress something upon my mind that was essential to get rid of this evil spirit. Again I commanded it to leave, but all it did was shake his body and make his face distorted. The man was semi-conscious when I had commanded the demon to leave, and he thought it was going to leave. Why didn't it leave?

We talked for a while and it was getting late. I told him my stomach was kind of irritated. He knew I liked ice cream and offered some vanilla to settle my stomach. I accepted and sat at his kitchen counter. He sat in the dining room about ten feet from me as I began to eat the ice cream.

I had been eating the ice cream for less than five minutes when a most unusual event began to unfold. Brad looked at me with a startled look in his eyes, and suddenly I knew why. Behind me was a bright light starting to fill the kitchen. It got brighter and was shining past me toward Brad. His mouth fell open, and the demon in him let out a scream and left him.

Wow! We were astounded at what we had seen. Jesus, the light of the world (John 8:12), revealed His light in a unique way to drive out the demonic power of darkness. He did it without us doing or saying a thing. It was wonderful to see God's "light of deliverance" (John 8:12) bestow mercy upon Brad. We rejoiced and talked about it. I finished my bowl of vanilla ice cream and drove home in peace with a smile of appreciation on my face for my Lord Jesus. Definitely, this deliverance taught me to b more patient with God's timing.

Teaching: I assumed that since a demon manifested I was to cast it out. Prayer for God's will should have been my focus, because sometimes a demon will surface just to agitate you or watch you waste your time. The Lord Jesus is always in control and proceeds in His way. His brilliant light of deliverance for Brad occurred over 30 years ago, and I've never seen this happen again. During each deliverance session, we must allow Jesus to work in His way.

Case 36: He Slithered to the Floor

My evening quiet time was interrupted by a phone call for help. Three friends wanted me to drive across town to see what was happening with a person who was showing bizarre facial expressions. They were convinced this college student they were sharing the Gospel with had a demonic problem. As I drove, I began to pray for wisdom, the anointing of the Holy Spirit, and for protection for all of us.

Upon entering the house, I was introduced to Jason. As he looked at me, his eyes began to close and slant, and he would not look directly at me for more than a few seconds. Sitting on a couch, I began to explain the Gospel to him, and as I did he trembled and became more agitated. He began to move away from me and slowly slipped to the floor.

What happened next shocked all of us. Lying face down on the carpet, Jason's body began to slither like a snake. He didn't slither around the room but just made the slithering movement in one area. Within a few seconds after the slithering began, a hissing sound came out of his mouth.

At that moment, I began to rebuke the demon. It resisted for a while then left him. Jason's face came back to normal. We talked and he received the Lord Jesus as his Savior. In Jason's case, there was no evidence of occult participation, so we never found out how this slithering/hissing demon had entered him. Jason roomed with a steadfast Christian, so it was easy for him to get involved with a fellowship.

Teaching: When the word gets out that you help people with demonic problems, the phone can ring at any time as it did that night. You must be ready to pray, counsel, discern with Christ's help, and rebuke the demon activity as directed by the LORD. You should also be open to explaining demon activity from the Scriptures to those who called for help, and make sure the former demoniac gets involved with a solid Biblical church. Delivered people need acceptance.

Case 37: Demons Dropped Through the Ceiling

Relaxing at 9 pm on a Friday night, we had uninvited visitors drop by but they didn't use the front door. There were four of us just fellowshipping when suddenly my friend sitting next to me and I saw some small demons drop through the ceiling and land on the couch beside the two people we were talking with.

As we continued our conversation, we noticed that the demons were speaking into the ears of our friends. Within a minute, both began to yawn and were looking sleepy. I looked at them and told them I knew why they suddenly had become sleepy. Then I rebuked the demons that had dropped through the ceiling. They disappeared and quickly both Christians were wide awake.

We discussed how they had been so alert, and within a minute they were yawning and sleepy. Now they knew why. Our conversation at the time of the demonic entry was about demon activity among Christians. It is disappointing that so many Christians think of demons as functioning *only* in areas of sickness, counterfeit miracles, various witchcraft practices, and violent tantrums.

Demons are smart and will influence their enemies (followers of Christ) to waste time as often as possible (Ephesians 5:15-17). They have been around for thousands of years and have studied humanity for the purpose of deceiving them in any way possible. Putting a stop to an evening of fellowship with "a spirit of stupor" is an effective way to limit growing in the grace and knowledge of the Lord Jesus Christ (2 Peter 3:18).

Teaching: A mistake made that night was not starting our time with prayer, because we knew our topic of discussion would be about helping the demonically oppressed. One of the people there had been delivered from a generational witchcraft background and was now a Christian. More than once, I have seen this demonic stupor impact people at different Christian settings. People forget that demons have the ability to work through dulling or partially blocking our senses. Jesus taught us a lesson that night. It's hard to pray too much (1 Thessalonians 5:17).

Case 38: A Disagreement Brings Deliverance

Visiting people I help who are demonized is common for me, because I look forward to encouraging them and developing friendships for life. One afternoon I went to visit a man who was not completely free of his indwelling demon activity. As we talked about a concern I had for him that I felt would quicken his road to freedom, he began to disagree with me. He had not acted in this manner before, so I carefully observed his face.

I was easily disturbed by the way the conversation was going, and I sensed a demon was working through him to agitate me, but he did not know it. So I asked him: "If at any time during our discussion I discern that a demon is causing a problem, would it be okay if I cast it out?" He said "Yes."

My next words were: "In the Name of Jesus I command the demon who has been speaking through him to be gone!" It took about two seconds for the demon to come out of his chest and disappear through the ceiling. He let out a gasp as he saw it come out of his chest. He asked me how I knew the demon was speaking through him at times. I told him that he had *never* been strongly resistant to anything that would help him with Jesus.

Teaching: Be prepared whenever you know you will be in the presence of someone who has a demon. Demons listen to what we say and figure out how to discourage, irritate, or harass us. They hate those who invade their kingdom of darkness with the kingdom of Christ's light. Build a relationship with the person you are helping so that they will trust your judgement over theirs. Be sure to always listen to what they have to say. There have been times when the LORD gave wisdom to a demonized person to humble me and encourage them in their battle for freedom.

Case 39: He Sought Satan for Athletic Power

I had become good friends with a former witch who now called upon Jesus as her Lord. Abigail gave me a call and asked me to come over to meet a longtime friend of hers who had a special need. The day was set, and I went to her place to meet a man with a great concern for his younger brother.

George was not a Christian but knew his younger brother, Jeff, had made a bad decision. He told me Jeff had made a pact with Satan for athletic power to be successful in college football. Jeff's goal was to have a career in the National Football League. Here are the details of Jeff's transition from a good football player to one who would suddenly possess NFL talent, talent that had not been shown previously on the field.

Jeff was 6 feet, 6 inches tall, and weighed 240 pounds when he played two years of community college football. Though he received a scholarship to a Division I school in Utah, Jeff was not as dominating as he felt he should be, and he wanted an NFL career. He encountered some people who told him that demons could give him strength and power in sports.

After listening to their information on "witchcraft athletic power," Jeff made a pact with Satan by signing a piece of paper saying he gave Satan power to control his life. He wore a leather necklace with a small leather pouch hanging on it. Inside the pouch was his contract with the Devil. The new power in Jeff's play was evident. He now was 260 pounds of demonically charged power. His defensive line ability got him drafted, and he played in the NFL for a few years.

When Jeff came back to his hometown to visit family and friends, George saw the leather necklace and pouch on his neck. He asked his brother about it, and Jeff told him the truth. George was shattered that his brother would make a pact with the Devil for power and success. George knew Abigail had been a witch and was now a Christian, so he sought her help. Thus, Abigail called me to combine our experience and together we would provide help.

George was desperate to help his brother. During our discussion, I asked George if he was a Christian and he said "No." The Gospel was explained to him, and he gave his life to Jesus. We continued talking and explained to him that prayer was the most effective way to change Jeff's mind. We prayed that God would send a person of influence to Jeff with the Gospel.

Teaching: It was explained to George that he must pray for Christ's protection whenever he met with his brother, because the demon activity in Jeff would sense the Holy Spirit power now indwelling him. Using demonic power to excel in athletics should not come as a surprise to Christians. Many Christians believe when it comes to any competition such as academics, job interviews, or athletics, it is wise to pray that the LORD would annul all demonic influence which could be involved to change the outcome of the situation.

Case 40: Her Little Girl Got Cursed

Another phone call from Abigail would bring another opportunity to glorify Jesus. She said a single friend had called from San Jose and asked if her two year old child could have had a curse put on her. Being a former witch of much experience, Abigail knew this was possible when the covering authority (father, mother) did not honor Jesus as Lord and Savior.

The lady drove from San Jose to Fresno. Our discussion focused on why she thought her little girl might have a curse on her. She detailed an angry, mean-spirited exchange she had with a witch who said she would put a curse on her child. Since that time, her child had not slept well and was easily disturbed. A point of interest was that from the time she entered the apartment, her child made an effort to avoid me.

The lady claimed to be a Christian, but was leading a life of sin. With no spiritual protection for her child, this probably was the opening the witch needed. It was explained to her that she needed to commit her life to

Jesus and get back into the Bible or the problem would not be eliminated. She confessed her sin.

We decided it was time to pray for her child, but the little girl started to run from me when I went to pick her up for prayer. The mother caught the child and held her against her shoulder. As I went to put my hands on her head, she reached up and tried to pull both hands away. The three of us were quite surprised with the arm strength the child revealed.

I said the following: "In the Name of Jesus, I take authority over all the demon activity connected with this curse upon (her name), and I rebuke and annul all its works." Within a few seconds, the child was relaxed in her mother's arms. The room was peaceful. We prayed some more and put her down.

This same child who did not want to be near me when she first saw me, or didn't want me to touch her, now accepted me. She came to me and enjoyed being around me, and didn't mind when I gave her a hug. Jesus provided the authority as needed. Mom and daughter went back to San Jose happy and free.

Teaching: You might object that a loving God would not allow a witch to put a curse upon a little girl. However, the parental covering is essential for protecting our little ones. There is no verse teaching that parents can lead a life of sin, and Jesus will automatically protect their children from all demonic afflictions.

Pharaoh's decree to kill the innocent male firstborn of the Hebrews "was permitted" by the LORD (Exodus 1:15-22). Also, Herod ordered the death of children who had done no wrong to him (Mathew 2:16-18). These events are painful to reflect upon, but the sovereign God does as He pleases and works all things according to the counsel of His will (Ephesians 1: 11).

Case 41: Demons Entered From Sexual Encounters

We had gathered to pray for a Christian man who previously had a demon cast out of him. He was seated on the carpet, and as we began praying for his freedom he flattened out on the floor with facial contortions, shaking,

131

and went unconscious. A few minutes passed, but there was no evidence that all the demons had left.

One person said that we should be quiet and see how God would direct us. It was quiet for about 20 seconds, and then we were taught a memorable lesson by the Holy Spirit. Out of the unconscious man's mouth, three separate demons told where they entered him and how they entered him. They said they had entered him on his trip to France when he had sex with different women.

I commanded the demons to be quiet. Then I asked the man about his trip to France and his sexual encounters. He wanted to know how I knew this, because he had never mentioned any of his French sexual encounters to anyone. When I told him three demons said it while he was unconscious, he admitted it was true. Shaking considerably, he confessed his sexual sins, and the three demons left him without being commanded to leave him in Jesus' Name. Repentance is amazing for removing demonic inhabitation.

Teaching: We did not take the time to pray and see what areas of counsel for repentance we should have pursued before beginning our prayers for deliverance. A background travel check would have been in order for this man, because he had told us of his travels and interest in France, a country not known for its modesty. Asking God to reveal all sin that has a demonic connection in setting the captive free is a must for Holy Spirit power to lessen the spiritual battle time.

Case 42: A Green Demon and a Purple Demon

Spending time with my parents in the past was enjoyable. They are now with Jesus in Heaven. One weekend I decided to visit them and sleep in my old bed to relax and bring back wonderful memories. After food and fellowship, I got into bed for a night of rest, but demonic spirits had something planned to disrupt my sleep.

I had been asleep for less than an hour when I was awakened by voices at my bedside. Two demons about five feet tall, one purple and the other green, were standing less than two feet from my bed. They were deciding how they were going to oppress me that night. I had opened my eyes just enough to see them. Then I shut my eyes completely and composed my thoughts as to how I should respond.

A few seconds later, I rebuked them in Jesus' Name. Instantly they disappeared. I spent some time in prayer and had a restful sleep.

Teaching: This evil visitation came unexpectedly. Prior to bed, I had not prayed specifically for Christ's protection from the evil ones. This taught me to take special time requesting protection for myself and all in any households where I would sleep in the future. Most of the time my request for protection has been honored by the LORD. However, at times demonic agitation has been permitted to alert me to pray more because of a tough spiritual battle that was coming. Prayer is an area where we can find needed improvement throughout our life.

If you are wondering about the colors of the demons at my bedside, you should know demons can manifest in a variety of colors, shapes, and sizes. I have seen them expand to more than twice their size and change their shape after coming out of a person. These spiritual beings are not limited to the physical dimension as humans are.

Case 43: Love Casts Out a Demon

Hume Lake, California, is a beautiful Christian camp for families to visit, for conferences, for various retreats, and for anyone who desires to spend time with Jesus in His eye-pleasing creation at 5,200 feet. What happened at a men's conference on a weekend was told to me by a close friend who had been used occasionally by Jesus to cast out demons.

A deeply troubled man with a demon came to a men's conference one weekend. He was indwelt with a demon. People had tried to cast this stubborn demon out but had no success. There was a man, known for his love, at this conference who heard of the man with a demon. He saw the demonized man standing alone and staring at God's Hume Lake beauty. The man of love went up to this suffering brother, put his hand on his shoulder and said: "Jesus loves you."

With a mild yell, the demon left him. God's love from a disciple of love set the man free. So often we hear messages on faith, hope, and trust. But how often do we hear a message on love? I can tell you why we don't often hear messages on love. The content of love in 1 Corinthians 13 demands so much vulnerability from us, which allows us to be hurt. And then we must forgive. The main part of the fruit of the Spirit is definitely lacking in Christianity.

Teaching: Love never fails to please the Lord Jesus, our Lord of love. We need to conform more to His image of love. How this deliverance occurred had a strong impact on the way I counseled people and developed patient love with difficult cases that took months to finalize. Take time now to ask for Jesus to *increase* your desire to love according to 1 Corinthians 13. Look at the specifics found in verses 1-8, and see where you need His help. Christians are to live in a loving bond of unity as instructed in Colossians 3:13-17. Unfortunately, much of Christian media emphasizes the bond of money, instead of love.

Case 44: The Demons Knew I Was Writing a Book

The man had gone unconscious on the carpet, and I was preparing to cast the demon out that had manifested. Before I could command it to leave, it blurted out the following:

> "We know about your book. You know too much
> about us. We won't let you get that book in print!"

This threat caught me by surprise. I told the demon he didn't decide the future of the book, and I cast it out. Again, evidence from the mouth of a demon confirms they are aware of some things we are doing. The book the demon referred to is titled, *EXPOSED: The False Faith Healing-Prosperity Gospel* (2015). It exposes dozens of false teachings by false faith preachers concerning sickness and healing about Jesus. It also reveals how false prosperity preachers seduce people for donations.

In 2017, I released another book titled, *Are Word of Faith Televangelists Misleading Millions?* This book mentions several names of television men and women who teach false doctrines about Jesus and what His blood atonement represents. The books are available on Amazon.

A year after this encounter, I was in a town about 50 miles from where the demon had threatened to stop the publication of my book. A woman was demonized by what the husband described as a mischievous demon. Upon confrontation, the demon surfaced quickly, began to plead with me, and said:

> "Don't cast me out. I won't hurt her like other demons do. I just want to have fun in her. Let me stay and I will help you get your book published. I know how to persuade people."

Immediately I commanded the demon to leave and it was gone. Two different demons in two different cities in two different years knew about my book to expose their false gospel and their "doctrines of demons" being preached to millions of Christians around the world. One threatened and the other tried to bargain with me to disobey Jesus.

Teaching: Even if demons know what we are doing for Jesus and cause problems, we are overcomers and succeed with His Holy Spirit power (1 John 4:4). And don't worry about what demons are permitted to see. Focus on Jesus (Colossians 3:1-2; Hebrews 12:2-4). Do the Lord's work (1Corinthians 15:58). "Trust and obey, for there is no other way to be happy in Jesus."

Case 45: Cast Out or Yelled Out?

Confronting demons can be tiring. It is easy to get extra mad at a demon that has resisted being cast out. In frustration, you can yell at the demon to "Leave in Jesus' Name!" thinking you have extra spiritual authority. But does fleshly anger have the power to cast out a demon and prevent it from reentering the person? The answer is found in a situation I observed.

A specific demon had surfaced and taunted both of us several times during a counseling session. It was commanded to leave but would not. It would go back down in the person for a few minutes, then it would suddenly manifest with its sarcastic voice and look at us with a wicked smile. In anger the pastor yelled the following: "I feel *compelled* to cast you out! Leave in the Name of Jesus!" The demon left.

However, the next day the same demon was back in the person. We were puzzled and wondered why it was back. The demon looked at us and said:

> "I know you are wondering why I am back. You didn't cast me out. I left because I didn't want to hear you yell at me anymore. Do humans like to be yelled at? No! Well, demons don't like to be yelled at. And when you said, 'I feel *compelled* to cast you out,' I knew you didn't have God's power to back you, so I left for a while. Ha!"

We agreed that our attitude was not led by the Holy Spirit, and that being *compelled* to cast out the demon was done in the power of our flesh of frustration. Repentance took place and the demon was gone.

Teaching: It's not uncommon to make "attitude mistakes" when casting out stubborn demons if you don't spend sufficient time in prayer and fasting (Matthew 17:14-21). We learned to fear God through repentance and more prayer time. We sought His guidance when we realized our mistakes were sins that allowed demons to stay. And we didn't ask this demon to tell us why he came back, but apparently the LORD forced him to tell us.

Case 46: A White Witch Who Liked Sex

As I continued to help people come out of the occult, the Lord Jesus was occasionally using these new Christians to persuade their former occult friends to talk with me about Jesus. These conversations helped me understand the mindset of demonized people, and enabled me to be more effective in presenting the Gospel to them. This is one of those situations, and it always provides pleasant memories.

A friend and former demon-indwelled person, who had become a Christian, set up a time for me to meet a practicing white witch. White witches normally use demons for health, love spells, financial help, or gathering information of interest. They prefer to call the demons "spirits" or "good spirits." Those involved with black witchcraft or the Dark Arts, use the evil spirits (demons) to curse people with sickness and varieties of mental and physical problems. This information about white and black witchcraft is not a stereotype of each. Witchcraft definitions and functions vary around the world.

We met with Carly at a restaurant in the afternoon, and she shared her occult lifestyle with us. She had a spirit guide and used him to attract men to her for sex. Recently an interest in the Gospel was in her thoughts. As a student at a community college, she made new friends in each of her classes. Some of these new friends were Christians who told her about Jesus, and the Lord Jesus would be moving into her life soon.

Carly said when she went to social functions, she would check out an appealing guy she wanted to know for the purpose of maybe having sex with him. She would "thought communicate" with her spirit guide beside her and tell the demon what to do. When she saw a guy she wanted to know, she would look at him and describe him to her spirit guide. Then the spirit guide would go to the man and whisper in his ear to turn around. When the man turned around, Carly would give him a big flirting smile. Then the demon would speak to the mind of the man and say something like, "Go talk with the woman who just smiled at you."

This technique worked constantly until one time when she really wanted to attract a certain student at a social function. But her spirit guide couldn't get him to turn and look at her. She asked a friend about this handsome guy who wouldn't look at her. Carly wanted to know *how* he could resist the influence of her spirit guide. This had not happened before.

The answer eventually drew her to the Gospel power of Jesus' love and His protection.

Her friend told Carly the guy her spirit guide couldn't influence for interest in her was a Christian. Carly was intrigued by this information. She began to look into Christianity and connected with a Christian friend who had been delivered from generational witchcraft.

Suddenly, in the midst of our conversation, Carly let out a gasp as we talked about the Lord Jesus. A demon had left her while we were sitting in the booth. The conversation continued. Carly realized her sin and renounced her spirit guide and all her witchcraft activity. She became a Christian, started reading the Bible, went to church, and spent time with Christians.

Months later she was doing well and moved back to her hometown. She continued her personal relationship with Jesus. Carly was such a pleasant person. I look forward to seeing her in Heaven.

Teaching: Because this young Christian student walked with Jesus, he would not be demonically seduced for sexual activity. We need more male and female Christians like him in the Body of Christ. His testimony of walking clean of his sins before the LORD drew a witch to repent.

Also, the testimony of Jesus from students she had met in her classes paved the way for the Gospel of repentance. Carly not only saw that Christians had greater power than a spirit guide (Jesus removed the demon from her in the restaurant without Carly asking Him), she heard of His love, forgiveness, and protection He gave to those who followed him. For her, the manipulation power of a demon was nothing compared to the loving power and forgiveness of the Lord Jesus.

Case 47: Demons Dancing in a Restaurant

It was Friday evening and four of us were going to have dinner at a nice restaurant. We sat in a specific food area in a booth. About 15 yards west of us was a dance floor with people dancing and a bar in the dance area. We had no interest in the music, alcohol, or the dancers. The music was not loud, our conversation was pleasant, our food was delicious, and we were sharing Christ's work in our lives.

Before we finished our meal, my attention was drawn to the dance floor. My eyes opened wide, and Jack asked me what I was staring at. I told him the LORD had opened my eyes to see small demonic spirits dancing above the people who were dancing. They were laughing, moving around the people, and whispering to them.

I asked the Lord Jesus to explain the purpose of what I was seeing that my friends could not see. In a moment, the Holy Spirit enlightened to know that these demons were planting suggestions of sin in the minds of the drinking dancers, suggestions that would lead to more drunkenness, various forms of sexual immorality, filthy language, and other sins for the night.

I shared this with my friends, and they agreed that various sins would be the outcome of many on the dance floor that night. We asked God to protect us from the evil in the place, finished our food, continued in fellowship, and had a good sleep.

Teaching: This was not a rowdy bar with wild music, yet there were plenty of demons dancing up a storm of evil less than 15 yards from us. We learned to always pray when we went to any restaurant, even one without a bar. You never know what kind of evil can be serving you or sitting around you. Pray for Christ's wisdom, protection, the opportunity to share Jesus with anyone, and that He would not allow any demon activity to follow you home. Give thanks and enjoy your spiritual and physical food. Tip for the glory of the LORD.

Case 48: The Little Girl Threw a Fork at Me

While talking to friends in a restaurant about demonic cases, a strange thing happened to me. A couple, with their three year old daughter, was sitting across the aisle from us. We had been in conversation less than ten minutes when the little girl picked up a fork, threw it at me, and hit near my chest. After the child threw the fork at me, she stared at me.

It happened so fast that the parents didn't have time to tell their little child to put the fork down. Quickly they apologized for her behavior, and said she had never done anything like this before. We knew that demon activity had used her for this bad behavior. Quietly, we prayed for the family and continued our discussion. At times, I would glance at the child and she had a blank look on her face at me, with no sign of embarrassment for her action.

Teaching: We had not prayed specifically before we were seated. It was daytime and mainly families were dining. There was no wild music, dancing, or drunks. You never know what is going on in the invisible spiritual realm. So always pray as led by the Holy Spirit.

Case 49: Retaliating, the Demon Rips Her Flesh

She had served Satan for decades, and now she had become a Christian. This experienced, former witch had used demons for varieties of gains and pleasures. Those who come out of long-term occult practices will agree that when demons are cast out of them or driven from their presence, demonic vengeance is not uncommon. This case reveals an extremely evil retaliation that the LORD allowed to come upon this former witch.

While preparing for sleep one night, Lilly sensed an evil presence had entered her bedroom. As she turned around to see what it was, she saw an ugly bird about the size of a large hawk with long claws suspended in the air. Before she could say anything, the bird sank its claws into her right shoulder and tore her flesh, causing her to bleed. Instantly the bird disappeared. She treated her wounds and went to sleep.

The next day she called me and told what had transpired. I went over to visit and console Lilly. She showed me the claw marks on her shoulder, and it was obvious these were thin-rowed narrow marks in a sequence that were not made by a human. Then she showed me the thin night gown she had been wearing when the attack happened. It had dried blood in the shoulder area, but there were no rips in the gown. There should have been torn areas in the thin gown Lilly had warn, but there weren't any. With no rips in the bloody garment she had been wearing, the evidence verified that a demonic spirit had ripped her flesh.

Teaching: Those who have had no experience helping witches come to Christ and have limited knowledge in what occurs in the "deep areas" of the occult, may find it difficult to accept that God would allow this to happen. I saw all the evidence, and it would be accepted in a court of law. Lilly quickly learned the importance of consistent prayer time throughout the day. Never did anything like this happen to her again.

Case 50: Evil from the Mormon Missionaries

There was a knock on my door. As I opened it, two Mormon missionaries wanted to talk with me. I invited them in to set them up for pointing out problems with their theology and their *false belief* that "the fullness of the everlasting gospel" is not in the Bible. They began their typical trained way of getting me to accept *The Book of Mormon* as a gift from them. I listened and began to make comments.

Within minutes, they realized they were in conversation with a person who had studied Mormonism and knew its weak and false points. Before they left, they asked me to take a copy of *The Book of Mormon* and read the testimony of their founding prophet, Joseph Smith. They showed me where it was recorded in the first few pages of *The Book of Mormon*.

I took the book so I could throw it in the trash, because it wages war against the truth of the Bible. As they handed it to me, I put it on the kitchen table. When they left, I opened it to the testimony of Joseph Smith and was astonished at what I saw. In less than three minutes, two words of "dried blood" had soaked into the testimony section of Joseph Smith. The words were blood underlined and said, "The truth." I tore it up and trashed it.

The Holy Spirit doesn't put dried blood on Bibles or other religious books to confirm they are true. We already know the Bible is the inspired Word of God (2 Timothy 3:16-17), and no other religious book is needed to supplement it. This "dried blood event" *only* could have happened with supernatural help from demonic activity.

My thoughts went back to months earlier when the LORD put on my mind to throw away a Jehovah's Witness *New World Translation of the Holy Scriptures* and *The Book of Mormon* that I kept. I had used them to show these misled people where their own books contradicted their beliefs, and this was unnecessary.

Teaching: This instant evil "dried blood" occurrence should be a strong reminder for all to not accept any literature or DVDs from those who do not *properly* accept the Bible as God's Word. When they have their own Bible translation, as do the Jehovah's Witnesses (*The Watchtower Bible and Tract Society*), that rejects the Deity of Christ, His physical resurrection, do not accept the Holy Spirit as a person, and the Trinity, you quickly know they are not followers of the true God. Thus, they do not bring the true Gospel of salvation.

If they have an extra book like *The Book of Mormon* that they say is superior to the Bible or a Bible supplement, it's obvious the true Word of God is not good enough for them. The Scriptures of the Old and New Covenant have been used for thousands of years. Anyone who believes the original God-inspired Scriptures are no longer good enough or sufficient calls God's prophets and Jesus a liar (Isaiah 40:8; 1 Peter 1:24-25). There is not one verse *in context* found in the Bible that teaches another "future book edition" will be superior and will be added to the Old and New Covenants at a later date.

I prayed and asked Jesus to remove any demons the Mormons left behind. Any time people come to your door to leave their sinful literature, don't take it. Immediately pray that God will remove any demon activity from all your property that came with them.

People involved with apologetics often have books from various cults for doing research to expose false doctrine. They should pray over these and ask the LORD to not allow demons to use these as contact points. They should also be open to the fact that God may not want them to have certain books for research. Spend time in prayer for Holy Spirit guidance in research and defending His Word (1 Peter 3:15; Jude 3).

Case 51: Sunday Morning Bible Study "Hiss"

The topic of conversation in our adult Bible study began to get controversial when the enemy's spiritual tactics were discussed. With clarity, I explained an area of concern to those in attendance to help them understand the context of the topic. As I carefully finished my insight, a woman next to me (a former witch) let out a "quick hiss" that was directed at me. It was loud enough for another man to look at her with a startled expression. He realized her "hiss" was not normal.

Teaching: It was clear to me that this lady had allowed a demon to "hiss" through her. This does not mean she was indwelled with a demon. But she was used to show that demon activity was present in the adult Bible study and was irritated by my Biblical explanation. At other times, people have blurted out something to me that was unnecessary or insulting in a Bible study. When this occurs, in my mind, I ask the LORD to remove the demon activity from our presence that worked through the person.

Always pray for the people who will be around you to repent of any sin *before* they attend church, a Bible study, a social gathering, or your home. Ask the Lord Jesus to impress upon their mind any sin they need to confess. Remember, the Gospels cite instances where Jesus cast demons out of people in the synagogues (congregational gatherings). Demons are not allergic to Bible studies, Christian homes, sports, school activities, or any denomination.

Case 52: Over 300 Years of Kahuna Witchcraft

Our Friday night Bible study had a new guest, and Jesus had a unique surprise for us. Carl had been invited to our Bible study by a devoted Christian girl he met on the Fresno State campus. As he listened to our prayers and Bible discussion, it became obvious that he was getting more agitated. His eyes darted back and forth, and they became partially shut and slanted in appearance.

When the study was completed, some got refreshments and a few stayed with me by Carl. Conversation continued and Carl was asked to read from chapter one of Ephesians. Before he had read half way through it, he slapped the Bible from his hands and said: "Get this shi_ out of my hands!" We knew a demonic battle was inevitable. This was the beginning of more than a year of Jesus calling me to develop a friendship with Carl and at times cast demons out of him. I will cite some of the deliverance sessions that took place during Carl's road to Jesus as his Savior.

I began to spend time with Carl and we became friends quickly. I liked him from the first day I met him. Before moving into deliverance, a reason for deliverance had to be discussed and accepted by Carl. When he shared his Hawaiian background and how Kahuna witchcraft had been passed down in his family and practiced for over 300 years, I immediately knew this would be a powerful stronghold to tear down.

He agreed that Kahuna spirits were demons. He had taken a specific Hawaiian name at age seventeen for initiation, and that allowed a certain Kahuna spirit to enter him and function in his life. There was a line of demonic healing that was to be passed on to him, as well as multiple divination powers. This deliverance would take months. Eventually, Jesus used a man from Colorado, who was more gifted than I, to set Carl free.

Carl asked Jesus into his life on a specific day in the month of May that he remembers quite well. This may shock some of you, but with the entrance of the Holy Spirit, all the demons were not immediately driven out. This began to wreak havoc for the demons in him, and he was determined to be free. He would not be denied freedom, grew in Christ, and persevered through much turmoil. Next, details of demonic resistance.

Bacchus, "the god of Wine"

Carl liked beer and wine, so it did not surprise me one night in counseling when a demon spoke through his voice that was linked to Carl's drinking episodes over the years. It identified itself as "Bacchus, the god of wine." Bacchus is also known as a "god of agriculture." I commanded Bacchus to leave Carl "in the Name of Jesus," and he left without a lengthy resistance. Carl threw out all the alcohol from his residence.

Teaching: Alcohol can open a door for demons (Ephesians 5:15-18).

Renouncing His Hawaiian Initiation Name

When Carl told me of the name he took at age 17 to open up his life to the Kahuna spirits for more power, I knew we must get rid of this "doorway spirit" that allowed other demons to enter. He renounced the oath he took to invite this specific spirit into him. (I have chosen to not mention the name of the demon that entered him at age 17). By name, I commanded the demon to "come up in the Name of Jesus." In a couple of seconds, it manifested through his face and sneered at me. Then it was commanded to "leave him in the Name of Jesus and to *never* enter him again."

The demon yelled and did not want to leave but was removed by the Holy Spirit. Carl felt relief that he no longer had any connection with or any obligation to the ritual/initiation demon. He reminded me that these demons we were fighting against would be trying to gather forces from Hawaii to come against us. So we spent time in prayer.

Teaching: Always check with the person needing deliverance to find out if there ever was an initiation or request for a specific spirit at a certain time. The longer the occult generational family line, the more likely a name will be given at a certain age to allow diverse demonic spirits to enter the person. Such rituals keep the evil power increasing in the family line.

Three Spirits of Divination

We were relaxing at his house one night when Carl remembered divination was to be a part of his Kahuna power. A spirit of divination manifested and it was cast out. We thought that would be the end of divination problems in his deliverance, but we were wrong.

At another time, Carl's face began to distort, and I realized a demon was looking through him. The demon identified itself as "Divination." This made no sense to me because the spirit of divination had been cast out. I called the demon a liar, and it looked at me and laughed. I went to the LORD in prayer to seek an answer.

145

After quiet time in prayer, something came to my mind in the form of a question. Could there be another spirit of divination in him? I looked at the demon in manifestation and said: "In the Name of Jesus, I take authority over *all* spirits of divination and command you to come out of him!" Two different demonic spirits of divination came out of Carl. Both of us were surprised that *two* more demons of divination left him. Carl was called to have multiple occult powers that were "layered" so that he would have special Kahuna powers.

Teaching: At this time in all my deliverance experience, I had never encountered a person indwelled with more than one spirit of divination. When working with demoniacs, who have had multiple powers passed down, it is wise to be sensitive to the Holy Spirit's guidance and not presume a person has only one evil spirit functioning in a specific area.

The Genuine Gift of Tongues is Evident

Leslie and I were visiting with Carl. She is a wonderful Christian woman whose lifestyle clearly represents the Lord Jesus. As we talked, Carl began to tremble. A demon appeared on his face. I took time to pray.

I looked at Carl and commanded the demon in manifestation to leave him, but it didn't. Again I commanded the demon to leave, but all it did was shake his body. Somewhat perplexed, but not ready to quit, I tried again to cast out the demon but with no success.

Gently, Leslie touched my shoulder and said, "Could I help?" I said, "Yes." She looked at the stubborn demon and in a Polynesian dialect began commanding the demon to leave Carl. The demon became furious and yelled these words at her: "Woman, you are disgusting! We will meet again!" and left. The Holy Spirit gave her this specific dialect that she had never spoken in her life to rebuke the stubborn demon in his native tongue.

You can think what you like about the gift of tongues, but this glorious occasion happened with three people as witnesses. What I couldn't do in English, the Lord Jesus did through Leslie in the demon's own Polynesian dialect. Jesus is Lord of the deliverance!

Carl was slightly conscious when Leslie spoke in the Polynesian dialect to cast out the demon, and he recognized it because of his background and trips to Hawaii. We spent time joyfully thanking the LORD. Leslie is one of the few people I've met in 44 years with this gift from the LORD. Later, she went to the mission field in Nairobi, Kenya and also did missionary work in the United States of America.

Teaching: Demons are cast out by the power of the Holy Spirit, not by self-determination. It is the will of God, not the will of man that secures the victory. It is by His Spirit great things are done (Zechariah 4:6). Once again I learned when a demon pops up in front of me, it doesn't mean I am to be the one to take authority over it and cast it out at that time. Demons are sneaky at getting those working in deliverance to waste time.

"Just Some Friends"

It was a night of friendly conversation when unexpectedly Carl slumped to the floor. A demon looked through his eyes at me for a few seconds. Then he looked at the ceiling with a smile. I looked up at the area of the ceiling where his eyes were focused. The demon said to me, "Just some friends." His friends were demonic spirits that quickly dropped through the ceiling and entered Carl before I could command them to leave.

Dismayed, I sat and wondered why God had allowed this to happen. What was the lesson in this event, because I had no intentions of casting out demons when I went to visit Carl?

Teaching: Always be spiritually prepared when spending time with a person who has demonic problems. It is wise to pray in advance that the LORD will not permit any demons to interfere during counseling or while dealing directly with demons when helping the person. Ask Jesus to not allow demons to call for reinforcements or have any communication.

A Den of Demons

When helping the oppressed, no evil object can be overlooked. I asked Carl to look through his house to see if there were any evil items that needed to

147

be destroyed. Our room to room journey led to a red square paper hat worn for sun protection by field workers in China. I picked it up and looked at the Chinese words on it, wondering what they meant. Carl had no idea what the words meant in Chinese. He bought the hat as a souvenir while vacationing in China.

An ugly look came upon Carl's face. It was a demon and it started snickering at me. The snicker became continuous laughter. Then it said: "A den of demons and he wore it! Ha!" I realized the demon was referring to what was written on the hat.

Teaching: Objects with any demonic connection must be destroyed Acts 19:18-19). The hat was destroyed and the mocking demon was cast out. Another unusual "item discovery" was waiting for Carl.

What is a Poi Pounder?

One day Carl was cleaning his garage and rearranging things when he ran across a Kahuna object he had forgotten he owned. It had been in the family line for many decades. It was a "poi pounder." A poi pounder is a basalt pestle that is used to crush taro roots (some refer to taro as kalo). The paste that comes from the kneaded taro root is filled with nutrition. Traveling Alli (royals) have had their own poi makers for hundreds of years, and it is a distinguishable Hawaiian stone implement.

There was a knock on my door and it was Carl. He showed me the poi pounder he had found while cleaning his garage. He came in and explained to me how and why it was used. He said after it was used to make a poi paste, the paste was offered to Menehune spirits for work to be done as requested in the fields of Hawaii.

The Menehune spirits are well-known in the Hawaiian Islands. No one who knows the heritage of the Menehune would ever say these spirits are not real. Kahuna priests honor them with poi and use them for specific needs. Carl had seen definite evidence of Menehune work in the fields.

Carl wanted to dispose of his personal poi pounder so I got a hammer for him. We went outside and he tried to break it, but it wouldn't shatter.

As he tried to smash it, a demon manifested in anger on his face. The demon was trying to stop him from smashing the object, but Carl wouldn't let that stop him. Still, only a few small chips were broken off of it.

He renounced any connection with this special poi pounder that was passed down to him and threw it in a large trash bin. As this was done, the demon left him.

Teaching: Again the importance of removing and destroying all occult connection objects is confirmed. A specific demon was connected to the use of that poi pounder, and was waiting for the time when Carl would pound some poi as an offering to demons. The poi pounder can be used in other places besides Hawaii.

These Kahuna Spirits Waged War: Kamehameha, Pele, and Kukailimoku,

This night was one to remember, because multiple strong demons would surface to resist being cast out. We knew it was inevitable that we would face demonic spirits with Hawaiian names because of Carl's background. For some reason, (perhaps his Hawaiian heritage) they were allowed to stay toward the end of Carl's deliverance.

As Carl began to shake and show signs of being controlled by a demon, we watched as a demon surfaced. The demons, who are mentioned in this example, seemed to have pride when proclaiming their names. Kamehameha is known as "the god of sorcery." Kulailimoku is known as "the god of war." Pele is known as "the fire goddess," and is linked to volcanic island problems according to Hawaiian history.

Individually and continually, each demon was commanded to leave Carl. One by one, they were cast out, with Pele being the last Hawaiian-named spirit to leave. As Pele surfaced, she began to make a sound out of Carl's mouth that sounded like pressured steam coming out, similar to what gases sound like when coming out of the ground during a volcanic eruption. The Name of Jesus put a stop to this demonic steam sound. Pele shook him around for a few minutes, then the Holy Spirit removed her.

149

Carl was very relieved. We prayed and thanked the LORD for His mercy. During this time, when these Hawaiian-named demons surfaced, Carl's face would take the shape of a Tiki god. The Polynesian Tiki gods are featured on Tiki poles, also called Totem poles by some. His face would become so distorted. It looked like a Tiki god found on the pole carvings in Hawaii. On one occasion, his jaw was elongated so much that I prayed quickly to Jesus to not let the demon tear any facial tissue. God answered my prayer.

Facial distortions that conform to the spiritual image of a demon are common. I have seen pretty women become so ugly when a specific demon manifested. As soon as the demon was cast out, the normal beauty of the woman returned. Also, I saw the face of a white witch, who was average in appearance, change to be very attractive when the demon "Pathos," the god of passion, changed her face to seduce men. Pathos was cast out. But this woman was not fully repentant, so I broke off counseling with her and told her to seek another for help.

Teaching: When helping those whose historical background is rooted in a generational occult belief as a lifestyle, it is common to find evil spirits with names tied to the culture. Therefore, pray that the Lord Jesus reveals all demons who are involved. Have the one seeking deliverance renounce any type of recognition ever made to these cultural evil spirits. This includes attending spiritual ceremonies and displaying objects to recognize any spirits. Even before casting out demons, you can ask the LORD to remove demons in accordance to His will (1 John 5:14-15).

With prayer, ask Jesus to *annul* the family line demonic powers that could combine for resistance to fight against being cast out.

Hawaiian Harlotry Was Hiding

Spiritual growth and more peace were taking place in Carl's life, and he looked forward to Christian music, learning from the Bible, and attending church. It was a joy to see him relaxed. Yet he sensed something was still wrong within him, and he shared his concern with me. I was beginning to

150

tire spiritually from this ongoing demonic confrontation, and I wondered if I was the person God called to finalize this deliverance.

We knew of a man from another state who was coming to Fresno. He had been used by Jesus to help many more demonized people than I, so we got in touch with him before he came to Fresno for an evangelistic outreach. We phoned him, and a time was set up to meet with him for counsel when he arrived. Before meeting with this man, time was spent in prayer for Carl's deliverance.

He was scheduled to speak at the fairgrounds that evening, so we met in a private room at the fairgrounds in the early evening. As the three of us settled in chairs, the man began talking to me and Carl for details about the situation. Within a few minutes, demon activity started shaking Carl. The man said, "In the Name of Jesus, who are you?" The demon replied, "I am Hawaiian Harlotry."

The evangelist asked me if I had ever encountered this demon in Carl. I said "No." The man commanded the demon to be bound in Jesus' Name until he dealt with him after he finished his evening message.

A few hours later, after his message, we went back to the room where we had first talked, and this is the way Hawaiian Harlotry was addressed. The man said: "Hawaiian Harlotry, you are no longer bound in Jesus' Name. Come up and show yourself." The demon manifested quickly, and the gifted man cast it out of Carl. Finally, freedom! The LORD had used me for months, and used this man for minutes to help Carl.

It was wonderful to see the completed deliverance work in Carl. He continues to follow the Lord Jesus. This commitment for Carl took over a year, and it really drained me. The demonic oppression I endured was only sustained by God's grace. I spent time talking to the LORD, and I asked Him if I could have some time off from working in this explosive spiritual area of ministry. His answer was conveyed in this way; for about two months, no one called me for help with demonic problems.

When I was completely strengthened again, I told the LORD that if another person needed help, I was ready to serve Him and help the needy.

He would again send a person my way. It would be the most explosive demonic case I would ever encounter, and it would take more out of me than Carl's lengthy situation did.

Teaching: This man was chosen by the LORD to uncover a cultural stronghold that I had not addressed thoroughly. (Promiscuity is common where demons are rampant. Ephesus and Corinth are Biblical examples of this). He was anointed for this deliverance to do what I had not been able to do. After various Kahuna demons had been cast out, I should have sought the Lord Jesus to make any demons left inside of Carl to leave. With one demon left in Carl, I am thankful Jesus did not allow others to enter him before Hawaiian Harlotry was cast out.

Also, if a person has the name of a demonic spirit, it does not mean he/she is indwelled with a demonic spirit. I know a young man whose first name is Damien, but there is no evidence he has a demon named Damien in him. Presumption has no place in deliverance help (Psalm 19:13).

In this next case of information, I will present the most intertwined case of demon activity I ever encountered. Some of the horrible things the pastor and I saw might seem hard for you to believe, but we saw them, as did the Lord Jesus Who granted amazing grace to this woman.

Case 53: A Phone Call from Oregon

Life again was smooth and calm. My time was spent working out, sharing the Gospel, gathering with friends, playing some tennis, reading the Bible, listening to pleasant Christian music, and doing personal research on Bible topics of interest. All of my needed time for growth and recovery would now be challenged with a request from a pastor in another state.

Casually I picked up the phone and a concerned pastor from Oregon introduced himself. He was in desperate need of help for a young Christian woman in his youth group who was heavily demonized. They were seeing some results with prayer and commanding demons to leave, but there were many demons in this woman. She had an extensive occult background, and the demonic resistance was strong. He had asked for help from two

Christian colleges, but they did not have knowledge of any one with experience in casting out demons.

He had a friend who taught at a Christian high school, and called him to see if he knew of anyone with experience in deliverance. The teacher was *the only* person in the state of Oregon who knew of my work with demoniacs. He knew that I had spent over a year helping a friend of his in California who had severe demonic problems. Mack gave my name to the pastor, and a connection between me and the pastor was made that would produce a lifelong friendship.

After talking and discussing the ongoing demonic problem at his church, the pastor offered to fly me to Oregon. I told him I could not come for about two weeks because of my carpet cleaning contract with stores. He said he would wait. Then they had another prayer session for the woman and more demons were cast out. It appeared that she was free.

When I called to tell him I would be driving to meet with him, he said there was no need for me to drive 12-13 hours to help finalize the deliverance. But I had been given a dream since I had talked with the pastor, and I knew the woman was not free. I said I would come, meet with him, and help set up disciple and growth guidelines for the woman. The pastor agreed.

Carl went with me to help. We arrived on a Saturday, and the next day we met with Pastor John. During our conversation, John stated that *when* Tammi received Jesus into her life, abnormal things began to occur such as resistance to prayer and trance like facial expressions at Christian functions. We attended the evening service where he pastored. After the service, we met in the counseling room and were introduced to Tammi, the woman who would spend dozens of hours in counsel and deliverance for the next nine months before every demon was cast out.

When I had been introduced to Tammi, she would not look directly into my eyes. As I began to ask her questions, she became nervous and this bothered the pastor. He asked me to stop, and just as I did, a demon manifested. The pastor said, "This is EAP. We thought he was cast out." I looked at Pastor John and told him I knew before I came she was still demonized, but he would have to see it for himself.

Tammi told us that when the demons saw me arrive they said, "Oh no. He's here." Why would they say that? Did they know God had a specific person to finalize her deliverance? Whatever the reason, the pastor, his wife, and I were called by Jesus to be the main "ministers of love and faithfulness" for months to help this woman. It would be a grueling, draining, and unpredictable time of battling strong demonic forces that had been in the family line for several generations.

EAP (Edgar Allen Poe)

We started with the demon named EAP (pronounced ep). This was an unusual name, but we can't expect demons to have everyday names we have heard for years. He was commanded in Jesus' Name to tell what his name represented and his function. He proudly stated *his initials* were found in an author's popular literature, and that he had influenced Edgar Allen Poe in some of his gloomy and depressive writings.

Tammi struggled constantly with depression. We talked to her to see if she had any Edgar Allen Poe literature, and if she had penned his poetry style with her writings. We found both in her room. Poe's literature and her poetry, which were inspired by her obsessive study of Poe, were destroyed. With the "physical" contact points gone, I thought EAP no longer had a "right of sin" to stay in her. Yet Jesus permitted EAP to stay.

I was also told that Tammi's dad preferred to call her Tamma, as did some of her friends. The difference between these two names (Tammi and Tamma) would later prove to be a deep generational "Druid problem" that was tied to the numerous demons we would face for almost nine months. Through information given to us by someone who knew Tammi's history and a vivid dream, we were given insight to the bloody Druid witchcraft on one side of the family that stretched back 20 generations to Ireland.

Pastor John had told me of the burnt Bibles they found at the fireplace in the youth room at the church and the blood that was on and around the

Bibles. Whoever or whatever entered this room more than once entered through locked doors. Later we would discover some bizarre occurrences that could only be explained by supernatural demonic invasions.

John also told me of a frightening event that took place at his front door shortly after he and another pastor at the church began praying for Tammi and casting out demons. One night in a trance, Tammi walked from her house to John's house with a large knife in her hand. She beat on his door, but it actually was the demon working through her. A demon was screaming in rage and threatening John. She was in a trance and had no idea of what was occurring. John called the police and they responded.

Growling from her mouth, the demons would not let Tammi put the knife down so a policeman smacked her forearm to knock it loose. This made the demon in manifestation even angrier. Finally they were able to get the knife out of her hand. Tammi came out of her trance, was shocked at what had happened, and did not remember ever getting the knife and walking to John's house. This episode made the local newspaper.

Teaching: The disposal of Poe's depressing literature would begin a process of removing many evil items demons had hidden in her room over the years. These items included vials of animal blood that were destroyed, as well as letters from "friends of sin." Evil communication produces sin and corrupts the Christian lifestyle (1 Corinthians 15:33) and can bring demon activity to those seeking deliverance from evil. We also looked at other books she had, and if they had no direct content that led people to Jesus or glorified God, we destroyed them. Tammi always cooperated.

The invasion on the pastor's house with a knife alerted us to the fact that more attempts to injure us were possible, and that the demons might try to inflict bodily harm to Tammi. Over the months of counsel and prayer, they caused much harm that drew blood and scarred her body.

"Your God Has Won"

As we prayed and began to help Tammi, the LORD caused a very unusual thing to happen. One day while in counsel, Tammi slowly slumped to the

155

floor. Within a few seconds she looked up at us and said: "There are three demons the LORD has told to leave me now." Two demons came out quickly without us saying a word. But one demon was still in her. Why?

Before the last demon left, our answer came in these words with a deep voice: "Your God has won." Then the demon left. But it would be about nine months before Tammi was set free from all indwelling demons, and we had no idea how difficult this would be. Passing God's test of commitment was not easy. It caused division in the church and startled her family.

Teaching: You are probably surprised at how a trance demoniac was told by the LORD what was to happen concerning three demons destined to leave. We were too, but it was a delight to see the LORD do it. The admission of defeat by this demon was very meaningful, because on two separate occasions we would fast for five days. During the succeeding months, at times it seemed little progress was being made.

We watched a young woman desperate for help being put on hold for months by Jesus. We saw scars left on her body by wicked evil spirits, and she had horrible nightmares. At times, the demons would put her in a trance and she would end up in another part of town. Some days she thought she was at school, but no teacher marked her present. Fulfilling his threat against me five years earlier, Damien, the son of Lucifer, had appeared to her and was causing problems. It was constant *Hell* for her. Yet she kept coming to us for help.

She Wakes Up to a List of Sins

Tammi called the pastor and asked for us to come to her house to see what had been left on her nightstand. When she awoke, her eyes were directed to a paper with a list of previous sins she had committed. She did not write these and had no idea how they got on her nightstand. We reminded her that in a previous counseling session that she had confessed these sins to Jesus, and He had forgiven her and would not bring up these sins to her again (Psalm 103:12).

Then we told her that this could only have been done by a demon to make her feel guilty and make her think Jesus had not forgiven her confessed sins. As soon as she accepted this truth, an invisible power began ripping up the sins on the paper right before her eyes. Yes, a miracle.

We explained to her that is how God treats our confessed sins; they no longer appear before Him. To Him, they no longer exist. A sudden burst of joy came on her face. Now she was truly convinced all her sins were forgiven. Jesus knew Tammi needed this for assurance and perseverance.

Teaching: Demons often try to make people doubt that their sins of repentance are not completely forgiven. This miraculous event generated new faith in Tammi, and it prepared us for more miraculous happenings.

Levitation and Slammed Against a Wall

Prayer and discussion were under way when two unexpected supernatural things happened. A wooden cross Lindy had given me after her deliverance was dangling down from my neck, and I decided to take it off as I read. Within ten seconds, it was picked up from the left side of me and tossed to the right side of me against the wall.

As we looked at where the cross landed, the chair Tammi was seated in slid quickly backward against the south wall. It slid back about three feet and remained there. Tammi was in a trance. We rebuked the demon activity and spent time in prayer. We knew the demons were trying to scare us with supernatural tactics, but our focus was not on what demons could do, but what the Lord Jesus wanted us to do. He is Lord of all.

Tammi was not injured, came out of her trance, and we continued our time of prayer and counsel. No other bizarre things transpired that session.

Teaching: Prior to meeting with a demonized person, ask Jesus to limit or stop all supernatural activities that demons would try to use for disrupting the session of prayer and counsel. If you are wondering why I said "limit," He may allow some things to happen to alert you to the intensity of the spiritual battle that awaits you. Trust in the LORD and He will guide you (Proverbs 3:5-7).

When something like this occurs, address the demons responsible for the activity firmly and command them to leave. If you ignore demons that do things like this and don't pray them away or command them to leave in Christ's Name and never come back, they will continue causing problems in your deliverance. Such events as this increase prayer time.

Sangthesin, "the god of Blood"

John had told me about a disgusting situation that occurred months before he called me. He said some ministers were gathered to pray for Tammi when a dark brownish, red-colored blood began manifesting out of her mouth. The demon responsible for this began spitting it on the men's shirts, their Bibles, and the table. He said the odor was terribly foul. They had to clean up the counsel room and were not able to cast out the demon.

On one occasion, Tammi walked into her bathroom and saw the words "KILL TAMMI" written in blood on the mirror. Blood also appeared on Pastor John's desk one time. We had prayed that Jesus would not allow the demonic blood to be put on Tammi's Bible and Jesus answered our prayer. She also wore a "Christian necklace" that the demons never touched. Yet, we knew the demonic blood issue would show up again.

While in counsel with Tammi, we saw her face get very pale, and seconds later we saw that ugly blood began to come out of her mouth. We commanded it to stop and it did, but the demon would not leave. Jesus did not allow any blood to get on us or our Bibles. We knew Jesus had a specific reason why He was still allowing that repulsive demon to stay, and when His reason was revealed, it was awesome! We would see the glory of God handle that repulsive blood demon in the future.

Teaching: This session prompted us to go to Tammi's room and look for any items that might have animal blood on them. We found some papers with blood used as ink for the words. The words were written in the Latin language. Tammi did not speak Latin, so we knew a demon had used her to get animal blood and write on paper. The papers were destroyed and no more bloody Latin writings were found.

As we looked through her room, which was a mess, we found three vials of animal blood. It looked identical to the dark blood that had come out of her mouth previously when she was in a trance. The vials of blood were poured out and destroyed. Even with these blood contact points removed, Jesus allowed the "god of blood" to stay.

Tamma Continues to Cause Problems

Since Tammi was called Tamma by her father from her earliest years, the demon named Tamma had cleverly intertwined her personality with Tammi's personality. This made it difficult to know whether we were talking to Tammi or the demon Tamma. This young woman had pleasant, light-colored eyes, but when the demon would look through her eyes, they would darken and almost become black.

And at times, there was a slight voice change, but it was difficult to distinguish a different tone. Sometimes in counsel or going through her room to locate occult objects, we would not realize we were talking to a demon that had mastered effective vocal deception.

Teaching: After discussing this intertwined personality problem, the LORD gave us this specific idea. We were to command the demon Tamma to separate itself completely from Tammi's personality, and never tie itself to the real Tammi again. When we prayed this, the demon was furious, because the Holy Spirit began separating the two personalities. Tamma now knew she had lost the invisible control she had enjoyed for years, and that her time of evil occupation was short. Quickly, we saw how our prayer was answered. Now, we were seeing the real Tammi more often.

Spiritism is Occurring in Another Room

Through Holy Spirit guidance, we found out that one of her siblings was also involved with witchcraft in a room where she lived. Her family was aware of Tammi's ordeal, so when we found out that a sibling in her house was talking to a demonic spirit on a regular basis, we were able to approach the person.

After a short discussion, the family member was convinced of the sin of Spiritism and renounced it. The demon never came back to the room to reestablish contact. Tarot cards were also found and destroyed. What is sad is that her sibling knew she was going through deliverance.

Teaching: When you are counseling/helping anyone with demonic problems, find out if others in their residence are participating in occult activities. If so, talk to them about the evil of it and try to bring them to Christ for salvation. Remember, this was a household where 20 generations of witchcraft had been passed down. Tammi was called in demonic prophecy to be a "High Priestess" in the Pacific Northwest area. The demons wanted as many as possible from her family to help them recruit other demon worshippers.

The Little People Were Real to Tammi

It was enjoyable getting to know Tammi. She was a nice person who didn't know she would be born in witchcraft. In counsel, we would not always talk about demonic problems. She was a talented athlete and very smart in academics, so we conversed in these areas. We worked at instilling edification in Tammi. This caused her to smile more and relieved her depression occasionally. To complicate her situation, the family was going through a difficult time, and her dad wanted nothing to do with assisting in his daughter's problem.

While meeting one day, the topic of not talking to any spirit that would appear to her and want to help her was mentioned. She looked at us and asked about the "little people" she talked to all the time while growing up. She had an Irish background, so we told her that the "little people" she talked to might be Leprechauns. She said they never told her about Jesus as God's Son. A spirit named Kūmba often appeared to her.

Teaching: The "little people" she talked to growing up were spirits whose job was to prepare Tammi to talk with adult spirits as she matured in Spiritism. This would make her more comfortable talking to various large spirits that would appear to her to grant her powers and guidance.

She Was Cut by the Demons

My involvement required that I would work for three weeks in California, and then drive to Oregon to spend a week. The intensity of the situation was increasing with physical violence. While asleep one night, Tammi was cut on her forearms with a sharp object we could not find. The cuts were deep and up to two inches long. Years later, the scars were still evident.

Also, while she was sleeping in trance, a demon pushed a pair of scissors in the bottom of her calf. When people are in a deep trance, it is much like being sedated for a surgery. They don't feel the pain inflicted from the demonic assault, but the damage done to their flesh will have pain in it after awakened from the trance.

Another time she went to a weekend youth retreat in the winter. She was wearing a flannel shirt to keep warm. Suddenly she noticed blood was coming from under her sleeves. She went to show John and she rolled up her sleeves. Upon careful examination, they counted over thirty paper thin cuts on both of her forearms, yet there were no cuts in her shirt sleeves. The demon(s) inflicted the cuts from inside her.

There is even more to tell about what she endured. Tammi called one morning, and said she woke up to find cuts on the front of her lower leg, some 2-3 inches vertical in length. Less than a month later, she was cut 2 inches across her mid-thigh, but it did not require stitches.

Teaching: Was this the vicious work of Sangthesin, the god of blood, or a different demon? It didn't matter what demon did it. We appealed to the LORD to put a stop to it, but He allowed more cuts weeks later.

Cold Air Came Out of Her Bedroom Vent

We went again one day to check for items in her room we might have overlooked. It was very cold, the type of winter day where people have their wood stoves, fireplaces, or house heaters going. The heater was on in Tammi's house. Entering her room, we noticed it was cold in there. I put my hand up to the vent where the air was coming out, and the air was cold. The other house vents had warm air coming out of them, so we knew this was the result of demonic spirits. Up to this time, no one had noticed the cold air coming out of her vent.

Teaching: We prayed and commanded the demons causing the cold air to stop their function. God answered our prayers. From that time on, Tammi had warm air coming through her bedroom vent.

A Demon Named "Lot"

A low sounding voice came out of Tammi and said, "I am Lot, and I have a lot of demons with me." I prayed, thought for a few seconds and said: "In the Name of Jesus, how many are with you?" Lot said over 500 demons were with him. For a moment I felt overwhelmed and wondered how this was to be handled. Then I prayed for Jesus to give us wisdom and guidance. Jesus gave us instruction in His way and it worked quickly.

Looking at the demon who was manifested on her face, I said to Lot: "In the Name of Jesus I command all the demons with you to bind themselves to you. When this is done, all of you will come out of her." About 30 seconds later they were gone. Tammi was permitted to see the work of the Holy Spirit as He bundled them to Lot for removal.

Teaching: It doesn't matter how many demons are with another demon for backup, because the Holy Spirit can wipe them all out in a moment of time. Depend on Jesus through prayer and He will guide you.

Demons Left and Came Back to Enter Her

The counseling session earlier in the day had resulted in some demons cast out. An idea came to us, something we had never considered. At times during counsel, we could see that a demon would leave without being cast out. So we prayed that any demon that left on its own to avoid being cast out would not be allowed to come back and reenter Tammi. Jesus heard our request, and that night His mercy was revealed.

Teaching: I felt led by the Holy Spirit to visit Tammi that same night. During our conversation, we saw "a stream of spirits" of different sizes come through her living room wall. I prayed. The room became cold. None of them came toward me. They went to Tammi, circled her and tried to enter her but couldn't. Within 30 seconds, they were gone. Assuredly, the LORD had impressed upon us to pray specifically that demons who left in a way to deceive us and then came back later would be kept out.

Walking in an 11 Degree Ice Storm

The weather report said an ice storm was coming from the north through Portland. I was staying at John's house with his wonderful family, and we were prepared for a cold night. We had been sleeping peacefully for a few hours when the phone rang. John picked it up, but no one said anything. He told me phone calls like this had occurred before when locked doors opened supernaturally for Tammi to enter the church to call for help. She would then be found in the church or somewhere outside.

John's house was a short walk to the church. We were there quickly. The main door, which had been locked, was open and that had allowed the phone call to be made from the church. We heard a distant voice coming from a field next to the church. In a demonic trance, Tammi was lying in the snow. She was wearing flannel pajamas and slippers, and had walked in the ice storm from her house to the church, a distance of over a half mile.

She should have suffered some frostbite, but any evidence of walking in an 11 degree chill factor ice storm *never* transpired then or years later. Tammi said she was aware of the walk, but could not stop it. She described something like "a bubble of light" that was around her "after" she was forced out of her house and walked to the church. Was this Jesus, the light of the world, protecting her? When we took her home, no one in her house even knew she had left. Jesus took care of her on that stormy, freezing walk in sparse protective clothing and kept her warm. This was a miracle. God is so good!

Teaching: Our prayers were answered that Tammi would not suffer any permanent physical damage from the freezing exposure. This unusual occurrence boosted her faith to believe that Jesus was always with her. In later times, when the demon activity would explode, she was reminded that

163

Jesus saved her life in a deadly ice storm. Therefore, He was not going to let the demons win this battle. She continued attending church, remained faithful in reading her Bible, always came for counseling, and at times showed genuine joy.

"Your Answers Are Found in Prayer"

We continued to devote many hours of counsel and time with Tammi. We were beginning to see more joy on her face despite the fact that God was permitting her to have unpleasant dreams at times. Also, the evil spirit activity around her was diminishing, but would come in like a storm at a later time.

After a counseling session that left us perplexed concerning what to do next for completing Tammi's deliverance, she took pen and paper and reminded us of what we must always do:

"Your answers are found in prayer."

We then realized we had spent too much time wondering what the demons might do rather than taking the time to pray, ask, and seek the LORD for His wisdom and guidance (Matthew 7:7). More prayer began to permeate our time together. And we would need it, because the LORD God was preparing us for a prayer time we would never forget.

Teaching: I had made three trips in three months to Oregon. During my 12-13 hour drive, I would pray, sing, and praise the LORD. But when I arrived at that little foothill church, I spent less time in prayer and more time in figuring out what the demons were doing or might do. What a mistake! Jesus knows everything in every situation. Come to the cross. Lay your burdens and spiritual labors down (Matthew 11:28).

Her Witchcraft Birth Mark is Exposed

During a time of prayer, Tammi brought something very important to our attention. While getting dressed that morning, she glanced at a specific

164

dark mark with an abnormal shape that had been on her abdomen for as long as she could remember. This is a common place for "occult birth marks" of those born in generational witchcraft who are called to have many powers. The occult culture sees this mark as a doorway for spirits to enter the body and soul.

I knew what *this* birth mark represented. The occult birth mark was explained to Tammi. She believed it was evil and renounced the demonic birth mark. At the time of renunciation, no demons manifested to fight. I do not know when occult birth marks are put on the person, but it doesn't matter. The blood of Christ cleanses all sin (1 John 1:7, 9).

Teaching: Some might reject that Jesus would allow a demonic birth mark put on a person. But remember, He allowed demons on different occasions to cut Tammi's skin several times. If you don't have a broad understanding of what the LORD allows demons to do (Job 1-2), and don't have many exposures to working with the demonized, don't attack the validity of this truth. Pray for Christ's guidance for those who are called in the area of ministering to people with demonic problems.

Damien Manifests at School and Church

I had received a vivid dream that Damien would be interfering in Tammi's case to cause various problems. I told John and we began praying for Jesus to prepare us. He appeared to her at school when she was on a grass field and put a "castion" in the ground for ritual purposes. She walked away.

Damien also appeared to her outside the church and in the stairway at her church. She rebuked him in Jesus' Name and he disappeared, but he would come back. At a later date, John came into the sanctuary and saw Tammi standing on the balcony railing threatening to jump off to the lower floor. The voice coming out of her was not her voice; perhaps Damien?

Being wise, John did not rebuke the demon, because this could have caused Tammi to lose her balance and fall below, which would have caused major or fatal physical damage. Instead, he read Ephesians 1 and preached a powerful sermon, so that both Damien and Tammi could hear the truth about Jesus. During this time, John was calling upon the LORD to protect Tammi from danger and asked her to step down from the railing. Eventually, she stepped down and was safe. Thank you Jesus!

Occasionally, for the purpose of fear, Damien would appear to Tammi as a solid-looking spirit to remind her he was going to be around to hurt her. We continued to pray that God would protect her and kept asking for the LORD to not permit any previous requests or bargaining from Damien to happen. We also asked Jesus to weaken Damien's power pertaining to possible future encounters. This was an essential prayer, because Jesus would protect Tammi and weaken Damien at the opportune time.

Teaching: From my previous encounter with Damien, I knew he would seek to cause complex problems with this deliverance. The fact that he had remained aware of my last five years of service to Jesus, followed me from California to Oregon, and appeared several times to Tammi, made us realize a confrontation with him was inevitable. But when?

The Demons Argued While in Her Body

While Tammi was unconscious one night, we heard two demons have an argument while inside her about what to do with her. One wanted to find a way to kill her. The other argued that they could get her back on their side to serve and worship them again. This disagreement went on for a minute, then they were silent.

We prayed for Jesus to protect her from death attempts by any demons and He protected her. Previously Jesus had protected Tammi during the 11 degree ice storm, so we had confidence that He was going to see Tammi through this tough time for His glory. Let the redeemed praise, worship, and serve Him!

Teaching: When the LORD God allows you to hear a demonic conversation like this one, it is very important to upgrade your prayers of protection for the demonized. No more bizarre, demonic death attempts were allowed before Tammi's holiday deliverance. We did not mention this dialogue to Tammi.

Jesus Gives Tammi a Beautiful Christmas Gift

Christmas was less than a week away. We sat down to discuss what our Lord Jesus wanted us to do next in helping Tammi have complete freedom from all indwelling demons. The same thing came to our minds as we sought what Jesus wanted for Tammi. We agreed that the Holy Spirit had put on our minds that we should fast and pray for five days to see what the Lord would do for Tammi. We were desperate to end this. The future victory would be found in prayer, fasting, and reading His Word

I had done three day fasts, so I knew this would be a challenge for us. It would be harder for Pastor John, because he had church commitments in music ministry and a family. Various liquids were acceptable. Our prayer-fast began on December 20th.

We continued to counsel Tammi and pray for the LORD to show how He was going to guide us during our fast and prayer time. The five days seemed to drag on for me. After day two, I wasn't hungry but wanted coffee and juice for warmth and energy.

On day five of the fast, we asked Tammi to come to the church for prayer. John, his wife, Tammi, and I were at the front altar area. The night slowly moved on with what seemed to be no progress to eliminate the remaining demons. We were praying and asking Jesus to help her, but nothing significant was happening.

I became frustrated and said to God: "We have been praying and fasting for five days. What do you want from us? We have been fighting these demons for months, and she's still indwelled with Tamma and other demons." My attitude was sinful. John's wife firmly and correctly told me that "This is not the time to be mad at God." She was right! Quickly, I confessed my sin to God.

Then in a few minutes I heard within my mind the following: "Stand up and tell Tamma to leave her." I obeyed and demonic Hell broke loose! Tamma began screaming "No" repeatedly, but her time had come to an end (Ecclesiastes 3:1). As Tamma was cast out by the Holy Spirit, He ripped her apart in different pieces to inflict severe suffering on her for what she had done to Tammi for years. Tammi was allowed to see this as the deliverance began.

Now, the authority and Holy Spirit power were there for us. I looked at a motionless body on the carpet and said: "All of you who are left, come out of her in the Name of Jesus!" One by one several demons exited through her open mouth. And Damien did not show up to fight us. Why? God's answer came months later. Finally it was over. Complete stillness was in the room. There was no evidence of any indwelling demons left in her. Prayer took place, with thanks to our Lord and God. The three month intense battle against numerous demonic powers was over.

It was past midnight, but we decided to go out for some food. As we relaxed and talked, Tammi told us something we have remembered for years. She said: "This is the first time in my life I can ever remember not hearing voices in my head." From her earliest years, when she played with literal Leprechauns, Kūmba, and talked with other spirits that eventually indwelled her, Tammi thought it was normal to hear voices or multiple thoughts in her head. She now was at peace with the LORD.

Teaching: When in difficult and ongoing deliverance situations, don't hesitate to fast with much quiet time in prayer. There was one thing that was a huge disappointment for the few who were involved for months in praying for Tammi. The church she attended preferred to keep her need quiet. It was like they were ashamed that Jesus had allowed this God-glorifying situation to surface in their church. To them this was a problem, rather than a blessing to deliver a life-long tormented person who attended their church. The elder board and other pastors showed little concern for the lengthy battle we faced.

For Tammi's family, things became more peaceful. No longer did the doorbell ring at various times of the night with no one at the door. Damien had been doing this. Nor were the stove burners suddenly found on with nothing on them.

Christmas was wonderful. The Christian holiday music was special to us. There was snow on the ground, and kids were sliding down the street on inner tubes, sleds, or plastic discs. Lights glistened with the help of the snow and various foods satisfied all. Tammi knew I liked fudge, so she made a big batch of fudge for me to munch on as I drove back to my home in Central California. Our rejoicing in her freedom would last less than two months, and we would be deeply grieved at what once again faced us.

Tammi's Ordeal is Not Finished

By phone, I kept in touch with Tammi to see how she was dong. For about seven weeks, things went well. She was reading her Bible, going to church, praying, listening to Christian music, and had support from some people who had been aware of her situation. She even had the courage to share her testimony to freedom with the youth group. And while working at an ice cream parlor, she was able to lead a girl to salvation in Jesus when business was slow. Fruit-bearing was evident (Galatians 5:22-23).

One night Tammi called me to talk. I could sense she was depressed and her speech flow was troubled. I thought this was an oppression attack upon her, which we expected. After talking with Tammi, I called John to share my concern with him. He had also noticed a slight gloomy change in her recently. Somewhat reluctantly, we discussed the possibility of Tammi being invaded by demons again.

The three months of counseling, prayers, and casting out of many demons had exhausted us, and he had a family that needed his time. John got back to me later and told me Tammi was again demon-indwelled. Another phone call from Tammi a week later confirmed she was again facing demonic problems. There was only one correct choice; drive 12-13 hours to Oregon and prepare for another intense demonic battle.

It was late February, and I told John I could be there to assist him in March. Both of us had no idea how Tammi could have been invaded by demons again. She was faithful and obedient to being discipled. This didn't make sense. She had suffered so much! Why was God allowing this? What was His purpose? Was there an area we had overlooked in helping her to prepare her armor for constant protection (Ephesians 6:10-18)?

We knew, with demonic reentry, the struggle for her freedom would be intense. The possibility of "new demons" entering her and obtaining knowledge from the others cast out could make it a fierce spiritual war. We remembered the importance of prayer and reading the Word out loud.

The hardest part of getting started was when we both had to tell Tammi she was once again demon-indwelled. She didn't want to believe it, because she clearly remembered the spiritual and physical hell the demons had put her through for over a year. The demons put her in a slight trance and blocked her mind from the truth when we tried to convince her that the demons were back in her.

We used taped conversations to convince her and asked the LORD to let the proof come through the recordings, and He did. Tammi's sobbing was crushing to hear. She wondered how much she would have to suffer again before all the demons were cast out. It was now time to let her mother know that again we had to face demon activity. The previous months of Tammi's battle had caused tremendous stress in her house.

Demonized Again: Where do We Start?

We talked and went to prayer for guidance. When the three of us met again to start Christ's path of light to victory, demons that had been in her previously boasted out of her mouth about their return. And we would encounter other demons we had not dealt with in the previous three month campaign of interceding for our precious sister in Christ.

Our thoughts went back to five months earlier when a demon said "Your God has won." We knew we had the victory, but did not know how long we would have to persevere this time before Tammi would be free. We knew the demons who previously indwelled her had studied our ways of help and would communicate with the new demons involved. This caused us to emphasize prayer, seeking the mind of Christ, reading specific verses that edified and strengthened Tammi, and Scripture for our edification. Also, we knew we might struggle with demonically-induced depression, if we were not careful with what we allowed in our thoughts.

170

We had found out that Damien hated the Deity of Christ, so we mentioned His eternal power and authority over all, which is mentioned in 1 Peter 3:22, as well as other Deity Scriptures. And the demons did not like 2 Corinthians 10 read out loud, especially verses 3-5. We prayed to break all new curses and spells that had been activated against us and Tammi.

The demons were doing something to Tammi they had not done before when we prayed for her. They were causing her legs and arms to feel burning inside her body. Prayer ended that discomfort. At another time, a small fire was suddenly started in her bathroom and in another bedroom in her house. Jesus put a stop to these fires.

"HELL" Was Scratched on Her Stomach

It didn't take long for the demons to let us know they were going to wreak havoc physically and mentally on Tammi. In a counseling session, she told us that on a Sunday afternoon "HELL," in two inch high letters, had been scratched on her stomach while she was sleeping and a knife had been stuck in her leg. The scratched "HELL" letters that drew blood were verified, and all of the scratches were visible for months. This was the last time demons were permitted to cut her.

Teaching: After months of prayer and asking Jesus more than once, He put a stop to the demonic cuts on Tammi's body. Many years have passed since the cuts, and some scars are still visible. We don't know why Jesus allowed so many demonic cuts, but He is Lord and oversees all (Hebrews 1:3; 1 Peter 3:22).

The Demon Was "Another Jesus"

We had been talking to Tammi about praying more. We told her to call out to Jesus for help, and she had been doing this when she was scared. During this prayer and counsel time, a demon popped up and spoke through her. It was commanded to give its name. The demon said "I am Jesus."

The demon said it had entered her when she kept calling out to Jesus for help. Sarcastically, it said, "Hey. My name is Jesus and she called out to Jesus, so I answered her call and came into her." He was cast out. This is strong confirmation of Paul's warning in 2 Corinthians 11:4 about "another Jesus." Demon activity is attached to the many false religions in the world that preach "another Jesus."

We explained to Tammi that when she called out to Jesus for help, she should address the real Jesus as "My Lord Jesus." There were no more problems with a counterfeit Jesus entering her.

Teaching: This information reveals that demons can hear our words at times. Solomon knew about open and curious spiritual ears that could be listening in the bedchamber (Ecclesiastes 10:20). The "bird of the air" mentioned in this verse is a metaphorical description of a demonic spirit. Therefore, be careful not to curse people (Romans 12:14). Your words of sin (curses) could be transported by a demon to the ears or thoughts of someone to cause problems.

Tammi Was Underwater in the Baptistry

Sunday services are often used for baptisms, so new believers in Christ can openly share their testimony of how they came to Jesus to have their sins forgiven. John's church had conducted a baptismal service the previous day. The baptistry had not been drained after the service. This case is another example which shows demons are aware of activities in churches.

John was finishing his work at the church office for the day when he received a phone call, but no one was on the line. The thought came to his mind to go into the sanctuary. His attention was directed to the baptistry, and he went over to see if it had been drained but it was full.

The baptistery had much more than water in it. Tammi's body was completely underwater and she was not moving. The water was smooth like glass, indicating she had been under the water for several minutes. John pulled her out immediately. She did not cough or spit up any water.

The demons had put her in a trance and placed her in the full baptistry to drown her, but her personal Lord and Savior, Jesus, would not let her drown. He did a lifesaving miracle to preserve Tammi while she was underwater. This is easy for Jesus to do when you consider how He parted the Red Sea for the Hebrews to pass through it (Exodus 14:21-30).

Teaching: Over the years, I have continued to thank Jesus for this miracle. And when baptisms are finished, drain the baptistry. There might be little children running around the church the next day and disaster could transpire. Remember the demon who argued out of her body and wanted to kill Tammi? Was this an attempt? If so, the LORD said "NO!"

He Boasted, "I am The Prince of Veils"

The prayer and counsel continued, and we were not surprised when new demons manifested. During an afternoon session, a demon looked out of her and said "I am The Prince of Veils." The function of this demon was to live out its name in Tammi to "veil" certain things from her mind. To me, it sounded like it said "I am The Princess Veils."

More than once I commanded "The Princess Veils" to leave, but the demon would not go. John corrected my misunderstanding of the name of the demon. Then I commanded "The Prince of Veils" to come out of her.

A similar situation had also happened before when I was casting out Hawaiian demons from Carl. He told me that if I did not pronounce the name of the Kahuna spirit properly, the demon would not leave. He was right, because on one occasion I mispronounced a syllable in the name of a Kahuna demon and it would not leave. Carl corrected me and the demon was cast out when I pronounced his name properly.

Teaching: If this seems puzzling or doesn't make sense to you, a different pronunciation of a name can refer to a different person. Demons have their own identity and respond to their name only. From this I learned not to be in a hurry or presumptuous. We asked the LORD to remove all veils of deception any demon had put in Tammi.

*She Brings Cocaine to Counseling

It was a cold winter night, a night when you are glad you have a warm jacket to wear. Tammi came for prayer, edification, and any help Jesus would give. The temperature was comfortable in the office, but Tammi kept her coat on. Suddenly, she reached into her coat pocket and pulled out some white powder that covered a large part of her palm. Instantly she put it in her mouth, gulped, and sniffed, and a demon made her go unconscious.

We knew it was not powdered sugar. Holding her wrist, Tammi's pulse was taken. Within seconds, her pulse was very high and she was going pale. A decision was made to pray for her pulse to go back to normal in one minute, or we would take her to the hospital. At 59 seconds, her pulse returned to normal, and Tammi came out of her trance.

Teaching: This was the third time demons had tried to kill her; the two others were in the ice storm and the attempt to drown her in the baptistry. During our months of prayer and counseling, we found out Tammi had attempted suicide before and had encountered several injuries growing up that required medical attention. Also, her parents had just gone through a divorce. Though Jesus would let the evil spirits afflict her physically and scare her, He would not let the demons kill Tammi. That evening, we had a productive counseling time.

*A Dream Provides Critical Information

In a counseling session, Tammi told us about a dream she had, a dream that would prove to be critical for prayer direction. In her dream, she walked into a room and saw twenty red-haired men sitting in separate chairs. As she entered, they all turned to look at her with an evil stare, and the dream ended.

We discussed the possible meaning of the dream. Since Tammi's ancestors had practiced witchcraft and one of her parents had Irish heritage, we agreed that the twenty red-haired men had a link to one side of her family. But why twenty men? After sharing possible meanings of the dream and praying, Pastor John said he believed the dream about 20 separate people represented 20 generations of witchcraft passed down to Tammi. We all agreed on this dream interpretation. Later we found out that Druid witchcraft was in her family line.

Teaching: The Holy Spirit gave us dream information that was needed. Tammi renounced all demon activity that was passed down to her through her ancestors. This broke the power of the twenty generation link, but did not remove all the demons. More prayer and rebukes directed at demons would cast them out later. This dream information also helped guide us to a specific prayer that will be revealed in the next heading.

*Retroactive Prayer

We were seeking the LORD on how to proceed in Tammi's ordeal when the words "retroactive prayer" came into my mind. A common definition of retroactive is, "made effective as of a date prior to enactment." We discussed how this could relate to Tammi, and we saw this as a word of knowledge from the Holy Spirit.

With understanding of this definition, we prayed and asked the LORD to go back in time and annul all demonic requests linked to this word from Him. As we finished the prayer, several demons began to scream out of Tammi and left. This prayer did not drive out all her demons, only the ones that had bargained with specific requests before God at a certain time in Tammi's past.

Teaching: When working as a team, it is important to share any unusual words or phrases that come into your mind. We were very thankful to Jesus for His "word of knowledge" help. Definitely, this word saved us many hours of counseling and rebuking demons. We should also remember that "retroactive prayer" is not to be used in every case. Tammi had several generations of witchcraft passed down to her to function as a high priestess. Therefore, we needed Christ's intervention to help Tammi. If you should encounter a case where generations of witchcraft were passed down to the person, seek the LORD for guidance to pray in this way.

*Uncovered, a Soul Sale in Blood

Tammi always helped us by going through her room to look for any forbidden objects. One day she found what appeared to be a "soul contract" with the Devil. Such a document gives the person's soul to the Devil in exchange for strong evil powers.

This did not make sense to us, because Tammi had been cooperative in seeking help from the beginning. If she was trying to deceive us, she would have kept the "soul contract" hidden. We discussed the situation and all came to the conclusion that a demon had falsified this contract, because demons have easy access to blood when they need it.

Teaching: Don't always assume every Biblically banned object is the result of the victim's free will to obtain it. Evil spirits have the supernatural power to make things appear in a way to deceive those who are helping. The handwriting on the "soul contract" did not match Tammi's. If you do end up helping a person who made a written contract with the Devil, burn the contract immediately when you find it. And expect a tenacious battle with demons, which will probably not end quickly.

*Jesus Protects Tammi's Bible and Necklace

During the many months of Tammi's time of pain and suffering, Jesus did something special for her. She wore a pretty Christian necklace honoring her Lord Jesus. In all the demonic Hell that took place, her necklace was off limits to the demons. It stayed on her neck and was not touched by any evil spirit. Also, the demons were never allowed to rip pages from her Bible. This was an ongoing sign to Tammi that the demons were not free to do as they wanted.

Teaching: Always ask Jesus to give signs of needed comfort to increase the faith of the demonized, which also reveals His love in a time of trauma. Remind the person that Jesus is in control of all that happens, even though sometimes it looks like He is letting the demons have too much freedom in certain areas that are painful.

The Pentagram Witch Sends Demons to Tammi

To complicate our situation, Tammi looked at us one day and told us a specific witch I had helped, but eventually turned away, knew of our battle and was sending demons to make it more difficult. I knew it was the lady from Texas who once stood in the Pentagram for initiation. She had also sent demons to interfere with Carl's deliverance. If you are wondering how Tammi knew of this, the LORD revealed it to her.

Teaching: Whenever you take the responsibility to counsel and pray for a person with demonic problems, ask the LORD to not allow anyone to send demons for interference. We prayed and asked Jesus to put an end to this harassment. He answered. And don't forget to ask the LORD to take His stand against the demons on behalf of all who are in prayer and praise for the person in need.

A Demon Named SLEAHC

Mistakes in confronting demons can follow you. Demons observe what we do and say for the purpose of becoming shrewder in future confrontations. This is an example of a blunder I made in anger and frustration months earlier in another deliverance.

In a previous deliverance, a certain demon was difficult to cast out, and he taunted me. Tired of demonic resistance, I looked at it and said: "Before you are cast out, you *will* confess Jesus is Lord! You might as well start practicing it now, because you will have to say it later when you appear before Him for Judgment." The demon resisted for a minute and then said through gritted teeth, "Jesus is Lord" and left.

We were relaxing in the midst of a deliverance session when a demon manifested on Tammi's face and looked around the room until he found me. He said "I am SLEAHC, spelled his name, boasted in what each letter meant as a separate demonic function, and sarcastically said:

> "Okay, you're going to cast me out, but before I go, you are going to make me say Jesus is Lord. Right? Okay, Jesus is Lord, but He is *not* my Lord! Satan is *my* Lord!"

The demon left. Pastor John looked at me, and I told him about another situation where I got out of the Spirit and into the flesh. I confessed my previous sin of frustration and trying to be Lord of that deliverance.

Teaching: I do not remember the specific time when I made a demon confess Jesus is Lord, but I know it was wrong. What this demon said shows they hear, know, and remember certain things that happen during deliverance times they can use against us in the future. Remember what Solomon taught us in Ecclesiastes 10:20. Only say what is needed to glorify God. Spend more time singing and praising the LORD.

Metaphisto, "the Wind Demon"

Pastor John called me about "a specific word" he had heard three times and wanted to share it with me to see how this word might be linked with Tammi's situation. While at home, he heard a word that sounded like "manifesto." But the third time he heard it in the stillness of his church office, he realized the word was "Metaphisto."

As we talked, I mentioned that I knew a former witch, who was now a Christian, and would call her to see if the name Metaphisto meant anything. Upon calling her and asking if she knew what Metaphisto meant, she quickly responded with: "He is the wind demon and comes with power." There was no time to waste. I called Pastor John, and told him I would be leaving that day for Oregon. My 12-13 hour drive was one of prayer and calling upon the LORD for whatever we would need to confront this demon, limit his power, and whatever accompanied him.

As I arrived and met with John, prayer and asking for wisdom were given to "the throne of grace" (Hebrews 4:16). We knew gracious Jesus had given us advance warning, with a needed word of knowledge, to prepare for this was a new demonic power assault to tear Tammi down. Pastor John called Tammi and set up a time to meet at the church. Despite the pain and suffering Tammi was undergoing, she was always eager to meet with us. If you are wondering why, it's because we complimented her on her obedience to Jesus, reminded her of progress, and we made it a point

178

to edify her with Scripture. We enjoyed seeing her and watching her grow in Christ.

In our next counseling session with Tammi in the church board room, we dealt with any demons that manifested. But there was no manifestation of Metaphisto. Our next meeting would be in the chapel room, rather than the board room, where we had met repeatedly. When Metaphisto entered the room to invade Tammi, it was to her benefit that she was seated on the carpet to cushion the demonic impact that threw her on the floor.

Prior to Metaphisto's entry, there was a weird stillness in the room. We had prayed in advance to prepare for what we had never experienced before. We knew evil was coming with power. Suddenly, we heard a sound like a strong wind. The sound came into the Chapel room, but did not swirl or throw things around. The sound went straight into Tammi before we could say a word.

Tammi squirmed as Metaphisto's power flattened her on the carpet. She was now in what appeared to be an unconscious state, but later she would tell us that Jesus allowed her to know what was transpiring. I commanded the demon to leave, but it would not go. Suddenly, Metaphisto began speaking out of her in an ugly demonic language for a few minutes. We couldn't stop it and when you find out why, you will be shocked.

After Metaphisto finished his demonic dialogue, the Holy Spirit gave Tammi the ability to resist that repulsive demon with a supernatural tongue (dialect). The demon had declared that he had a right to indwell her. But from Tammi's mouth came a strong rebuke to Metaphisto. She told him he had no right to be in her, and that he must leave her. The demon left her and the room was quiet. Tammi sat up and told us that she had heard and seen all that had occurred.

John and I were stunned at what we had seen and heard. In answer to our many prayers in advance, in which *we thought* we would directly confront this powerful demon, the Holy Spirit had us watch with awe and praise as He did the work. He had an amazing plan to eliminate Metaphisto from Tammi without using us to cast the demon out. He gave Tammi a supernatural tongue and authority to drive out the demon. Metaphisto never returned. To my knowledge, Tammi never spoke in tongues again.

Truly this is bizarre and hard to believe, but John and I saw it, and the Holy Spirit is our witness because He did it. There is no reason for me to fabricate this to impress you with the spectacular, because other strange and unusual examples of supernatural occurrences we saw have already been presented. If you read Numbers 22:22-33, you will see that the LORD caused an animal to speak to the prophet Balaam.

Teaching: When we realized Metaphisto was going to become involved with the demonic assault upon Tammi, our prayer time increased. We did not want this demon to enter the room and bring a powerful wind that could cause items to be swirled and knocked around. The LORD did not allow this demon to distract us with any wind. And no other demons were allowed to assist Metaphisto in his attack.

When you are helping demoniacs, do not treat any word lightly that keeps coming to you. Share what comes to your mind with all involved in the deliverance, and pray for Jesus to show you the purpose of a certain word or phrase that comes to your mind. Words of knowledge (1 Corinthians 12:8) are a vital, strategic, and powerful part of the Holy Spirit's help to accomplish the miracle of deliverance.

Sangthesin's Blood Disappears

Here we were again, resting near the alter area while Tammi was lying in a trance. Several minutes had transpired, and we felt led by the Holy Spirit to wait patiently for the Lord's next move. Tammi began to move, and Sangthesin made himself known by starting to produce blood out of Tammi's mouth. I reached for a cloth to quickly wipe it off her cheek and mouth.

Pastor John told me not to do this, but to watch what was going to happen. Suddenly the blood began to disappear from her face and then it disappeared all the way back into her mouth. As this was happening, the demon began to scream, "What's happening! Who's doing this?"

The Lord Jesus had seen enough of this filthy demonic blood coming out of Tammi's mouth. His Holy blood had been shed to forgive her sins, which she *had* accepted. Tammi belonged to The Lord of Lords and King of Kings, and He was displaying His sovereign authority and love for her.

Tammi's personal Lord Jesus intervened with amazing grace by making the occult blood disappear from her mouth, chin, and face. We watched in awe as the awesome God of all creation displayed His glorious love. We said nothing and the demon left.

Teaching: The evil, foul-smelling blood of this demon had been allowed to supernaturally manifest several times, but after God intervened there was never a blood occurrence again. We had continued to pray for Jesus to stop the blood, but we had to wait for His time. Philippians 4:6-8 is good news. Personally, I enjoy watching the LORD God Almighty remove demons from people, rather than casting them out myself. He does a marvelous job.

Legion Gets Cast Out

For months we had not been successful in getting rid of Legion. We weren't able to just call him up and cast him out. It was like he preferred to remain undercover when we were around and then wreak havoc at night in Tammi. Though the battle was never-ending, we sensed that the LORD was going to help us more in unique ways, because we were facing new demons and many of the old had come back.

We were very dependent upon His guidance, rather than all our previous knowledge. Apparently Legion was going to be dealt with by Jesus in a preset time. While we were lying down inside at the front of the church, praying and waiting for the LORD's guidance, something unusual happened. A demon began to speak in tongues through Tammi as it looked around to observe the surroundings.

Was it communicating with another demon, acting as a forerunner, or just evaluating the situation? When it stopped speaking, the atmosphere changed as another demon came up to look through Tammi. This demon seemed to bring a presence of power. God gave us discernment and Word of knowledge to know this was Legion. The confrontation we had longed for was now present.

At the time of agreement, we stood up and took authority over Legion and every demon connected to him, and there were many. We commanded them to all to be gone with Christ's given authority. Without resistance, they all left.

Teaching: In deliverances where there are many spirits and reentry from previous demons occur, patience and much prayer are a must. Ask God to give you as many of the 1 Corinthians 12:4-11 gifts listed that you will need. And ask Him to protect you from any counterfeit gifts or dreams.

Do not consider all information from the demonized to be wrong. We learned that Jesus gave Tammi much insight (even accurate dreams) to her situation and specific details that we had to know for success. Personal help from Jesus also made Tammi realize how much Jesus loved her when she was severely demonized during her lengthy time of ordeal. This helped her grow quickly in her relationship with Jesus.

What a Demon Admitted Before Leaving

An earlier case mentioned that Tammi had written down vital instruction for us to follow. Her words from the Lord Jesus to us were: "Your answers are found in prayer." This was a major factor in our victory. A few months *before* every demon had been cast out, a demon glumly said to us:

"Your prayers have ruined our plans."

After saying these words, more than one demon left her without a fight. Those called to minister to the oppressed must have an exceptional prayer life and must remember that in Christ's plan, there is a perfect time for prayers to be answered. Pray and persevere with holy patience.

Damien thought his attack would tear the situation apart. However, we prayed more than once that when Damien manifested in Tammi his power would be weakened. When it was time to face him, his power was weakened. It was nothing like my first encounter with him as cited in case 2. The Holy Spirit disposed of him. Jesus answered our prayers.

However, Damien was not finished with oppressing me. Less than a year after Tammi was set free, I was planning to head to San Diego for a week of carpet cleaning. Before I left for my 5-6 hour drive, I checked all the tires to make sure they had proper pressure. When I looked at the rear tire on the passenger side, I noticed that one of the lug nuts was almost completely unscrewed. As I bent down to tighten it up, I noticed two other lug nuts were also loose. This was no coincidence. In my previous four years of travel around California, no lug nuts had never come loose on my van. The nuts were tightened, and prayer for God's protection began.

After cleaning a store later that week, I was driving on the highway late at night when I heard what sounded like a softball had been thrown at the side of my van. The loud sound came from where the rear passenger tire was located. No other cars were around me. I felt a strange and evil presence in my van. I began praying for Christ's protection, and His protection would soon be needed.

A few miles down the highway, another demonic encounter would occur. Suddenly there appeared before me, in the middle of my lane, a young man. It happened so fast that I did not have time to brake. The man went right between the driver's and passenger's seats. There was no physical collision. What I saw was a demonic spirit. It was Damien. He was trying to get me to swerve at high speed to cause an accident.

About three years later, Pastor John was doing some janitorial work at the church. His attention was directed to a window. As he looked at it, he saw Damien looking through the window at him. Quickly he went outside to confront and rebuke Damien, but the demon disappeared.

EAP was also one of the major problem demons who had reentered Tammi. He was responsible for various demonic problems. Toward the final days of Tammi's freedom, EAP was forced up by the Holy Spirit to say these final words for God's glory before leaving:

"Jesus is the Victor and Lord!"

Demons know that the risen Christ is LORD over all situations. EAP left and never came back. His constant depression influence is gone. Tammi had tried to commit suicide more than once due to the demonic oppression from early childhood and had suffered several childhood injuries. To add to her depression, she was not treated well by some people close to her, and one relative believed all her trauma was for the purpose of getting attention.

But Jesus had a plan of love. She went to a church when she was five years old and later was baptized. In high school, she truly became a Christian. With the Holy Spirit entering Christ's redeemed temple, the explosive stage was set for a spiritual war that lasted over a year.

I have not listed all the hurt Tammi went through for years, but enough was listed to give God great glory for His relentless love to redeem her and deliver her from evil. She bears the scars of a spiritual warrior.

Her inner healing would take years, and Jesus had someone picked out in advance to love her, understand her, and help her spiritual growth. Tammi was married to a man within a year after she was set free from her multiple demonic problems. Her husband was a man who had deliverance experience and fully understood her unusual life from birth to the marriage altar. Jesus blessed them with four wonderful children.

There is another important piece of information that needs to be shared. There was a youth pastor (Joel) who worked with Pastor John, and he was the one who first discerned Tammi's demonic problem. He worked with her for around three months and left for another position at a church. She was sad, but Pastor John devoted extensive time to help her.

After Tammi was set free on Christmas Eve, I stopped by Joel's home in Southern Oregon to tell him of her freedom. When I told him that Tammi was free, he was *not* excited. He said he now doubted that she was ever demon-indwelled. I was shocked. He had been an eyewitness, yet Satan had tactfully blinded him from reality.

Furthermore, at the same church, there was an assistant pastor who worked with Pastor John for a one-time visit to help Tammi. He saw names of demons written in animal blood on pages of paper that she had in her room. Various names were written in "pig Latin" and English. Also, books were found under Tammi's bed that she had taken from the library. The books contained information (names) on various demons that were historically linked to the Druid occult line.

Tammi was inquisitive, ingenious, and wanted to find out what was behind the many Druid witchcraft names that were coming up during her deliverance. Upon finding the books, the assistant pastor thought Tammi's ordeal was a hoax for attention. He didn't care about the origin of the blood on her papers, nor did he want to help anymore with her ordeal.

As I look back over the years, besides myself, *only* Pastor John and his wife remember this ferocious demonic battle for a soul who was destined to be a "High Priestess" with generations of multiple supernatural demonic powers passed down for her use. All of the people who helped were oppressed by strong demonic power over the years, and their walk with Jesus didn't grow much. For me, John, and his wife, we chose to call upon Jesus repeatedly for strength and continual protection. This was needed, because we have faced many trials in our lives for years.

The demons were furious at any who helped Tammi. More than once they threatened to come back in the future to get back at us. They have kept their demonic word by harassing us in multiple ways over the years.

There were other lengthy sessions where demons were cast out of Tammi. I did not include all of the deliverance sessions we had the second time around and how we dealt with multiple demons, because enough information was cited for you to understand how difficult it was for all of us. Battling 20 generations of built up witchcraft powers was exhausting.

Other bizarre stuff occurred such as objects levitating, and Tammi being taken out of her body (astral projection) against her will while we counseled her or at night when she was at home. More prayer was needed to remedy the astral projection problem.

I am not exactly sure, how, or why the demons were allowed to reenter Tammi. One demon boasted about bargaining with God as found in Job 1:7-12; 2:2-7. Maybe he lied. God alone knows why the reentry happened. In all her brutal suffering, we *never* heard Tammi curse God or complain in a sinful manner.

This commitment wore me out, and my Lord Jesus has not called me to work in any extended cases like Tammi's since except for a haunted house situation. I remain open to serve Him should He give me authority again. A few times since Tammi's freedom, Jesus has led me to cast out demons. One more situation is important to explain, and not many are aware of this "occult secret."

"The Calling Out"

What is "The Calling Out"? This wicked calling pertains to Satan calling out, by astral projection, current occultists *involved* with blood sacrifices. It happens throughout Halloween night around the world. Horrible things (various rituals of abuse) transpire in this "spiritual realm event." Not many people know about this astral projection event that takes place only on Halloween after sundown. It encompasses special worship to Satan with various blood sacrifices.

Sometimes the intense Halloween oppression can be felt by those who have come to Christ and *were* once a part of "The Calling Out." Call on Jesus for peace and protection. More prayer time might be needed for certain Christians who were previously involved with this intense night of blasphemous satanic worship around the world.

In conjunction with "The Calling Out," the topic of Satanic Ritual Abuse (SRA) of people needs to be addressed. Some people believe Satanic Ritual Abuse does not happen. This belief is not correct, because the Bible records that the demon-worshipping nations that opposed Israel performed satanic human rituals of abuse in their cultures. Proof of satanic ritual fire abuse is found in Leviticus 18:21(Molech is a demonic god), Deuteronomy 18:10, 2 Kings 23:10, and Jeremiah 32:35.

The content definition of SRA includes those who are abused in various ways. It can include forced cuts on people as "a blood offering for power" to Satan, forced sexual activities, physical harm inflicted on others involved with the ritual, and other combined physical and verbal abuses designated by those in charge of the SRA.

I know an adult, now a Christian, who went through SRA as a child. She still has her spiritual struggles (fear) and like her husband has a tendency to blame demonic problems on other people. Both of them claim to have the gift of discernment but do not follow Scripture in certain areas. That is deception, not discernment.

Hollywood: "Hell is Very, Very Real"

Before I conclude this section on literal demonic situations, there is one more case I want to cite. I have this on CD and reviewed it on July 7, 2018. We were praying for a demon-indwelled man one night. As he slipped to the floor, he went into a semi-trance, meaning he could hear what was happening but could not stop it.

Before I commanded the demon to leave the man, the demon quickly said the name of a well-known actor who had died from an overdose a few months earlier. This shocked us because this man's name had not been a topic of conversation that evening. Here is what this guttural sounding demon quickly said *after* stating the man's name:

> "Had his chance. He sure did. You should see him now.
> Flames. He wishes he had another chance. He just laughed
> when people told him about Christ. He just laughed. It was
> beautiful. Ha, Ha, Ha. People think it's a joke. Ha! Wait
> till they come down herrrrre. Oh yeah, oh yeah. It's no
> joke. Hell's so real. Hell is very, very real."

We were stunned to hear this. The topic of Hell, as a future destiny for those who reject Christ's forgiveness, is seldom mentioned in church pulpits as it was years ago. In the future, all demons, all evil people who would not let God forgive their sins, and Hades will be cast into the lake of fire to receive "their free-will and chosen" eternal judgement (Matthew 25:41-46; Revelation 19:20; 20:11-15; 21:8). In the last quote, the demon referred to Hell's location as "down herrrrre" or what is called the underworld (Psalm 55:15; Isaiah 14:15). The saved are "up there" in Heaven with Jesus (Ecclesiastes 12:7; Acts 1:2; 2 Corinthians 5:8).

Earlier I mentioned that before I became a Christian, I tried to commit suicide. I saw a horrible place of darkness, and Jesus did not let me die. After I became a Christian, I was taken to a place to view where many were suffering in darkness and leaping flames. I was told that I was being sent to warn people about this horrible place that was reserving souls for the final "great white throne judgement (Revelation 20:11-15). In obedience to Jesus and love for you, I have supplied these accurate details as a warning of love from Above.

Concerning the information on these various demonic descriptions, I have been involved with all of them except the one of the deliverance power of Christ's love at Hume Lake, California. The facts were given for God's glory. They were not provided for excitement or entertainment, but to let you know that Satan and his demons are **"vicious soul hunters."** They want to devour people (1 Peter 5:8). Satan's main goal is to prevent people from going to Christ to have their sins forgiven, so that *the unforgiven* will live miserably in the lake of fire, suffering forever (Revelation 20:14-15).

Demons have extremely effective miraculous powers of deception and spiritual bondage. Proof of their demonic deception is confirmed by the many humanists, atheists, people involved with various witchcraft practices, and false religions of the world that do not believe Jesus Christ is *the only way* to Heaven (John 14:6; Acts 4:12). Make a commitment to read your Bible daily and to pray often during your waking hours. Establish sound doctrine, fellowship, breaking of bread, and prayers (Acts 2:42) as a way of life to honor Jesus as Lord and Savior.

To again substantiate the power of demonic deception, a detailed dream will be cited. The lady, who had this dream, was a God-glorifying Christian for over 20 years after she was set free from several demons. She was given a detailed dream instructing her to write a book about her difficult deliverance to freedom to help others. Her husband was willing to help her.

In the dream, she was in the family room of her house dressed in her beautiful white wedding dress seated at a table. Light was coming through the windows and shining all over her as she was writing the book. She would write for a while and stop to see what Jesus would put upon her mind. I have seen the room in that house, and it is a peaceful and spacious room with a nice view for calming effects.

Decades have passed, and she has not started the book and most likely will never write it to help many people. This is a tragedy, because this woman has forgotten what Jesus wanted her to do for Him and others. Probably some demons worked on her mind to block remembrance of Christ's desire to help multitudes with demonic issues. This shows the power of evil spirits returning to take vengeance upon a living human temple they once indwelt. It also shows what happens when Jesus is not given first place on a daily basis. I still pray this woman will one day write her book before she appears at Christ's judgment seat (1 Corinthians 5:10).

If you check back in all the cases I cited, you will see we never called upon Michael, the Arch angel, to help cast out the demons. Some people, who do exorcism rituals, ask for Michael's help, but Jesus and His disciples *never* taught this was needed when dealing with demons. Angels *are not* indwelled with the Holy Spirit for casting out demons. Christians *are* indwelled with the Holy Spirit (Romans 8:9, 11) for casting out demons "In the Name of Jesus" (Mark 16:17).

Many believe only Catholic priests, certain priests, or pastors are given the authority to cast out demons, but the Bible doesn't teach this. Upon conversion to Christ, all Christians are a holy priesthood (1 Peter 2:5) and "priests unto God" (Revelation 1:6). Therefore, Jesus gives authority to His chosen person(s) to cast out demons. This includes men and women.

Some also teach that holy angels do miracles and physical healings. They cite John 5:1-9 as proof for their belief. They believe that when the angel "troubled" or "stirred up the water," the angel did the healing. Verse 4 says the angel *only* "stirred up the water." This was a sign that God was going to heal the first person who stepped in the water. This verse does not say the angel healed the person. Gifts of healing come from the Holy Spirit (1 Corinthians 12:9). God's holy angels do not heal people. However, demonic healing spirits have the power to masquerade and heal.

Don't be deceived or misled by those who teach and instruct people to go to specific "healing pools" and God will heal them, "if they have faith." Jesus and His disciples never taught that miraculous physical healing pools would be established by holy angels or Christians in areas of the world. Healing witches know that healing spirits (these healing spirits are demons) can be activated for healing the deceived who place faith in water-selected areas.

Another false angelic teaching needs correction. Some believe people become angels when they go to heaven. The Bible does not teach this belief. Upon born-again conversion (1 Peter 1:23) to Christ, we become saints (Romans 1:7; 1 Corinthians 1:2; Ephesians 1:1) and holy priests (1 Peter 2:5; Revelation 1:6) of God, and we are *never* transformed to the nature of an angel.

If you think a departed loved one becomes an angel and is watching over you, then a demon can counterfeit the voice and personality of that deceased person and trick you into contact and conversation. Such a practice is Spiritism and is a sin. It will destroy your prayer life.

The topics of Yoga and Reiki healing stir up strong opinions. It might surprise you to find out that both of these have an occult connection. My book titled *Are Yoga & Reiki Healing Evil?* gives explicit facts from *their* websites to answer this question. You will be surprised at what is revealed by the experts in these two areas of so-called health.

People from various cultures and religions around the world have been indoctrinated with centuries of unbiblical influence. Traditions of sinful spiritual connections have created immense deception concerning Biblical truth. Scripture tells us to ask, pray, call upon, seek, beseech, and entreat *only* the LORD to have our sins forgiven and for any healing. Being humble and open-minded to Biblical correction strengthens and glorifies Jesus as Lord.

It was very painful to watch what demons did to these people. Years later, it still hurts to remember and write about what was seen. However, my inner healing is established through what Jesus, "the Name above all Names" (Philippians 2:9-11), did for these former demoniacs. I will end the numerous examples of demonic afflictions and doctrinal corrections by sharing a portion of Scripture from Romans 8:37-39 that we all should remember for strength and comfort:

Nay, in all these things we are more than conquerors through Him that loved us. For I am persuaded, that neither death, nor life, nor angels, nor principalities, nor powers, nor things present, nor things to come, nor height, nor depth, nor any other creature, shall be able to separate us from the love of God, which is in Christ Jesus our Lord.

Isaiah 40:30-31

Even the youths shall faint and be weary, and the young men shall utterly fall: But they that wait upon the LORD shall renew their strength; they shall mount up with wings as eagles; they shall run, and not be weary; and they shall walk, and not faint.

Casting Demons Out of a Haunted House

I looked at my phone screen and was happy to see the name of a friend I had not talked to in almost 30 years. What could be on his mind to give me a call? It was wonderful to hear his voice, and know that he and his wife still followed Jesus as their Lord and Savior.

Quickly, Randy got to the point. He asked me if I still helped people with demonic problems. I told him "Yes, as long as they commit their life to Jesus." He said there was a family that lived in a town near me. He knew they were Christians, and the husband had told him evil things were happening in their house. I was given their phone number and called them.

I drove over to meet with them and establish a friendship in Jesus, because we would need to be close during this demonic battle, a battle to my surprise that would take months to finalize. Bizarre descriptions of supernatural occurrences they provided in our initial conversation clearly confirmed there were demons active in their house. I explained my background with dozens of demonic encounters to them so they would know I could help them. I told them I would be with them until the demons were driven out.

Their son was sixteen and was not a Christian. Before the house deliverance was finished, he saw numerous examples of demonic things and some occurred in his room. Through all these terrifying evil events that will be described, he became a Christian.

All of the demonic supernatural events that will be cited occurred at daytime or at nighttime. My information comes from what I saw and notes taken by the wife (Loretta gave me dozens of pages of detailed notes about what happened). When you read all the demonic manifestations, you will be astonished at what these people faced for months. It was exhausting and frightening. At the end of our battle against evil spirits, their reasons for being resistant to leave will be given.

Their grounds for staying and fighting against us will tie in with the chapter titled *Ways Demons Can Enter People*. From that chapter, it will be shown exactly why the demons kept coming into the house after much prayer and fasting. You should know that the husband's former wife was a Mormon and mean-spirited practicing witch. It was also uncovered that Loretta's mother was a demonized person for years who verbally crushed two of her four children.

Before I met this family, the demon activity had made their life so uncomfortable that they were driven out of their house and spent three days in a hotel. From my previous demonic encounters, I knew this would be an intense battle for all of us. However, I had no idea it would take us more than six weeks to drive out the various demons that were sent from two evil sources, Loretta's mother and Allen's former wife.

When I first visited them, I was shocked at how much of a mess was in their house. I told Randy it was the messiest house I had ever entered. The mess would reveal a vital reason why demons had spiritual rights to come and go without restrictions, because the mess covered hidden occult objects. It would take weeks to go through the entire house, including the garage. In cleaning up their house, dozens of 35 and 50 gallon plastic garbage bags were filled with items stored for years that had never been unpacked from a previous house move.

Another reason it took so long was because both were working, and when they got home they were tired. Plus, he worked at night, and she taught elementary education. However, they did make an effort to work together when they had the energy. And because of lack of sleep, they both were tired during this ordeal.

The format for explaining this evil, horrific event will be explained by presenting a comprehensive list of the numerous ways the demon activity went on the spiritual war path against this family. The demons were relentless in progressing with various demonstrations of evil for months. They tried to instill fear and fatigue to wear us out. Keep in mind that two churches in my hometown were also praying for the demons to be cast out of the house. So please don't think it was lack of faith that delayed the expulsion of the many demons.

When Loretta's mother moved to a rest home near her, the stage was set for the demonic house invasion. Because of the years of verbal abuse, Loretta did not like to be with her mother. When Easter came, she chose to not visit her mother. Within a few days, a demonic presence began to display itself in the house with wicked and bizarre occurrences. This presence produced months of various demonic manifestations.

As Loretta's mother lie waiting to pass away, she said something that was quite revealing. She said: "Tell Loretta and John that I am sorry." She admitted she had mistreated and abused two of her four children, and knew she had treated her other two children well. John and Loretta remember the ugly energy they would feel come off of their mom when she was mad at them. Loretta could never figure out why her mother picked on her and John.

Upon checking the family history, there was history of rapes, incest, and sodomy. At least one adult knew of these while they were occurring and did nothing about them. He just let the victims suffer. Often these three areas have a direct link to the occult. Those who know of occult practices would confirm this.

When the funeral was held, I went with Allen and Loretta. John did not attend. One of the grandchildren spoke. He said he remembered when Grandma read scary stories, she would imitate the scary creatures in a way that scared him. John, who did not attend, said that when he talked to her on the phone, her voice would change to a harsh, raspy tone. Loretta said she also heard her mother speak like this at times. Voice changes like this are commonly found among demon-indwelled people.

Demons communicate in their spirit world as freely as humans communicate in their physical world. Demons can pass around information about people, and they can get together at times when planning to make humans suffer. This is what happened to this family. When Loretta's mother died, the demons transferred to the presence of her daughter. And at some point, the demons from Allen's former witch-wife connected with the demons around their house. Also, we later discovered there had been witchcraft involvement among her grandparents – some generational witchcraft was passed down.

Whenever more than one source of demon activity is in the battle, it intensifies the demonic power. During our demonic onslaught, we received information through a dream given to their son. James had never seen a picture of his dad's first wife. In the dream, he saw a woman standing on their front lawn, and she was sending evil spirits into their house. When James described her in detail, Allen knew it was his first wife. She was still cursing and spell-casting him years after their divorce. This definitely increased our prayer life.

Their traumatic ordeal began two months before I met them. I spent about six weeks helping them. You should also know that the family lived in their house eleven years before the demons erupted with violence. So they did not move into a haunted house, but it became a haunted house.

I knew from the description of the violent evil spirit activity that it would be important for me to sleep at their house for a night. We set up a time. I told them I wanted to sleep where the demons had been the most active. This is important because you get to see what the demons are doing, and it sends a message to the powers of Hell that you do not fear them. Some fear is common when facing off with an invisible force of deception. But fear must not occupy your mind to cause interference with God's will. And I knew from the descriptions of the violent evil spirit activity that we would need to work together.

They set me up on a couch that looked straight into the room of evil. I prayed, remained awake, and waited for what would transpire. It was clear to me, because of many demonic exposures, that the atmosphere of this house contained strong demon activity. Other than seeing a few demons come through the walls that night, it was not spiritually explosive. We spent time in prayer asking the LORD to rid the house of demons. I left for home, told them I would be back, and told them they could call me anytime for prayer or just to talk. I would receive several calls before the battle ended.

During this extended time of demonic resistance, I slept at their house three times, and on one occasion I fasted for three days. After the fast, it was peaceful for 2-3 days. Then the demons renewed their assault to win the battle.

I will now present a lengthy list of the numerous supernatural evil things several demons displayed in their house for almost four months. These will not be in the exact order and some happened many times. And some days were quiet. On numerous days, I would drive about 20 miles to help them, then drive back home to sleep.

Keep in mind that throughout this intense battle, the family played Christian music from their I Phones, prayed, had Scripture read to them from their I Phones, quoted Bible verses out loud, and played Maranatha praise music or other Christian music.

1. The family portrait was thrown face down in the hallway.

2. These noises began to occur: Thumping on walls, banging in her son's closet, hearing running footsteps in the hallway, walls being scratched, James's bedroom door would be constantly opened, and he had nightmares about Satan.

3. Loretta began to feel tingling sensations in different rooms that she had never felt before. Her legs would suddenly become weak.

4. Their Nest camera recorded the drapes blowing at night with the windows closed. Doors opened when no one visible was at the door, and lights were flashing off and on like fireworks.

5. Constantly the alarm would go off when there was no reason. They would reset it and again it would go off. I was there.

6. When sleeping on the couch one night, I saw the thermostat turned by an invisible force from 76 to 90 degrees in one second. This happened several times for weeks in summer weather.

7. A demon left three scratches on James's mid-back.

8. Also, a demon left three scratches on his calf. I saw them.

9. Televisions began to turn on and play simultaneously hard rock demonic music throughout the house. So we unplugged them, and the demons plugged them back in and played more demonic music. To top off their demonic dominance for evil music, they even turned on the televisions without them being plugged in. During this time, the remotes had no control over the televisions. We prayed often for Jesus to put a stop to this and He did.

10. Sometimes the demons would take the TV channel to an occult movie that was playing.

11. Allen's small TV was taken over in his room, and the Google pod came under demonic control.

12. Sometimes the language coming from the television was weird, not English.

13. The power to the fuse box was turned off more than once.

14. A poster of a love painting (not sexual) was thrown to the floor.

15. James's laptop was thrown across the room and damaged.

16. A light in James's room went from white to glowing red. I saw this. The evil spirits caused many malfunctions in his lights.

17. The demons stole Allen's Maranatha CD out of his boom box.

18. At times, it sounded like a train was crashing into Loretta's room.

19. Demons opened closet doors repeatedly, bathroom doors, and threw items on the floor.

20. Loretta's bed was shaken for long periods of time, making it difficult to sleep, and often her room was quite cold.

21. More demonic running in the hallways transpired.

22. The hallway was the coldest area in the house, yet there was no vent that allowed air conditioning to enter.

23. The mirror in James's room shook at times.

24. Numerous Nazi emblems/patches were found and destroyed. Any model or picture with a Nazi symbol (swastika) was destroyed.

25. A book titled *The Devil's Dictionary* by Ambrose Bierce was found and destroyed. They didn't know how the book got into their house.

26. Numerous pictures of Allen's former wife were found and shredded. Anything such as a genealogy record, or a diary record that was linked to "the witch" was destroyed.

27. Art and figurines that had ugly representations on them were crushed.

28. Lucifer match boxes were found and watered down before they were destroyed. Several were found in different rooms.

29. Loretta's medical kit was thrown across her room. No damage.

30. When working in the family room, they went to check on what smelled like smoke. On the bathroom floor were some burnt matches and some not burnt. They formed a pentagram. Loretta took pictures of all abnormal manifestations

31. The next day, while helping them, I went to the bathroom and found three candles burning on the tile. We threw them out.

32. Matches were often found in different rooms. They were soaked and eliminated.

33. James saw the face of a demon looking through the back door. This day of severe and persistent demon activity drove them to a hotel for the night.

34. Sometimes *all* the drawers in the house were opened.

35. Demons spoke through the three unplugged TVs and said "Get Out."

36. While sleeping there one night, a surveillance camera was ten feet away from me and a voice out of it said "Out." I commanded the voice to "Leave in the Name of Jesus." Then I got some sleep.

37. James came out of the shower and noticed some words were written in mist on the mirror. The words were "Get out." I told the family leaving would not solve the problem, because the demons would follow them or stay in the house to harass others.

38. They had double bolt locks on the front and back doors, and several times they found them unlocked, wide open, yet the screen doors remained shut.

39. Allen had purchased a small machete with a scabbard. One day the back door was opened and Loretta went to close it. As she got near the door, she noticed the machete was lying blade up in front of the door. It was thrown away on trash day. Allen then made a sticker for the door that said "Jesus is Lord." The demons pulled it off of the door, and the next night stuck it on the tip of her largest carving knife. This could have caused severe damage to the foot if stepped on. Loretta told the demons "Jesus wins." We bent the carving knife in a vise and threw it away.

40. One day, when James was in this same room, a glass bottle was picked up and thrown at the door where the machete had been. The bottle was shattered. The glass was cleaned up.

41. There were shelves in this room that had dozens of small jars of paint for Allen's art work. The shelves were knocked over three different times before the demons gave up. We would put them back up and pray.

42. The demons continued to speak with strange sounds through the Nest System to fatigue the family.

43. James got into the new Acura to leave one day. The car would not go over 15 mph for several minutes. Then it functioned normally. Another time James went out to drive the car, and it was moved diagonally on the drive way. This happened twice.

44. Sleep for Loretta and James was sporadic. Then the sleep deprivation hit Allen. The whole family was exhausted daily. God's amazing grace strengthened them for the lengthy battle.

45. At times, the demons would interfere with the functioning of James's computer, phone, and the Acura's sound system. Evil voices would talk through the Acura's speakers.

46. In the room where the demons wreaked more havoc, a can of beige paint was opened and poured on the tile. While they cleaned up the paint, the family's computer tower was thrown to the tile. When they went outside to dispose of the paint mess, they returned to find the floor covered in DVDs and papers. When the demons poured paint a second time, they spelled Allen's name in blue paint on the tile.

47. James would receive strange phone calls on his I Phone. When he answered, he would hear men's and women's voices screaming.

48. Under a stack of books in this same room, we found a powerful occult book titled *The Grimoire*. A friend had given it to Allen years ago as a gift. Allen never opened it. In ignorance, he just stored it.

49. On the same couch where I slept, Loretta was resting one day. She was shocked when it began shaking and it moved a foot. James saw this.

50. When James was cleaning out the garage, the shelves shook violently back and forth. The word "Die" was carved on two shelves. On another shelf was 666. Loretta and I saw these evil carvings.

51. More than once, the demons imitated the voice of Loretta's son to cause fear. They yelled "Mom. Mom" making her think her son was in trouble.

52. Loretta's mother was buried on July 9th, and on that day "I love you. Goodbye" appeared in the steam from a shower on the bathroom mirror. The house had peace for two days. Then the new strength of the demonic presence was evident. What was around the deceased was now around the daughter with hatred.

53. The demons drew a pentagram on Allen's bedroom floor with liquid laundry soap. It was cleaned up and they did it again.

54. Voices were heard talking in the house.

55. Individual demons would appear in spirit form and glare at us. One night Loretta and her sister saw a demon peeking under the bedroom door as they tried to sleep. Her sister showed her how to play Scripture on her I Phone. The demon left.

56. At times, as many as three demos would sometimes look through the window of the room where most of the supernatural events occurred.

57. One day at my home, I was listening to Maranatha Praise music on YouTube and suddenly a demonic rock group began singing through my computer. This continued to happen between praise songs so I switched to praise in Spanish. The same demonic rock group started singing in place of my Spanish praise music. I prayed and the demonic rockers were silenced.

58. Their little dog was found in a cardboard box in the summer sun. When they found the dog, it was in a box too high for the dog to have jumped in, and it was dehydrated. If not found, the dog could have died in the hot afternoon sun. The dog had been locked in a room while the fire department checked some concerns. They have four dogs, and they usually stayed with each other.

59. To complicate the ordeal, it was believed the neighbors across the street were practicing witchcraft.

60. My writing pen I use for notes was taken from the kitchen and put in the main room with demon activity.

61. A DVD Loretta gave to James that shows the Gospel of Luke was hidden. When found, a demon had put a drawing of a pentagram and 666 inside the paper cover.

62. More than once, a bathroom sink began to overflow from a faucet that no one turned on. This also happened with the kitchen sink.

63. One day, a trail of knives on the floor led to Allen's room.

64. Another day, the knives led to the back door where the demons had previously placed the machete.

65. Often, the drawers where the knives were kept was open. The purpose of this was to instill fear in the family. Also, one time when coming home, James saw every drawer in the house open and left when the demons yelled "Get out."

66. In another incident, six knives were laid at the back door.

67. Often the washing machine lid would be pulled up to stop the cycle.

68. A second time the words "Get out" were found on a bathroom mirror. The words had been spelled with a bar of soap.

69. Anything found that was connected to her mean-spirited and demonic mother was destroyed.

70. On a Sunday morning, Loretta woke up to find a 3 inch crystal in her bed. Not all crystals are evil, but some are used in the occult for magical powers.

71. Loretta's longest turkey carving knife was found on the floor.

72. A knife was found on the daybed where I slept.

73. When the house was being cleaned out, the trash was placed on the patio. Soon an unusual amount of flies, bees, and wasps were flying around us. I bought a can of insect spray.

74. James was bombarded with bad dreams for months.

75. When going through various items for disposal, Loretta found her mother's Bible. She had no idea how it got into their house, and she would not have kept it if her mother had given it to her. Later James found it in the garage with the carving knife placed in the Gospel of John. John's Gospel was the book Loretta would play on her I Phone to get rid of the demons.

76. Items on the kitchen counter were moved or new items were placed on the counter when they were not home. Things were found in drawers that did not belong there.

77. Several times the surveillance cameras showed a person, not a spirit you could see through, walking in the house.

78. On August 1st, we found our last occult object, an evil book, and destroyed it. It was hidden behind some history books on a shelf in Allen's room. He had no idea how it got there. The book is about a religion that wants to destroy Christianity. Peace ensued.

79. Before I had met them, they had anointed their house with oil and walked around the yard asking for God's blessing to put a shield of protection around their property. I also anointed their house with oil and prayed.

80. When we were about half way through this battle, Loretta told her pastor about this situation and told him he could call me. He never called me or dropped by to pray for the people in desperate need.

There were more demonic issues than what I have listed, and some of those listed were constant, such as the evil presence felt almost continually for 3-4 months. Can you now see why this was not an easy battle? We had to oppose a practicing witch who kept sending demons to the house. We had to break generational bondage because demons had been passed down, and we found so many Bible-forbidden objects to destroy (Acts 19:18-19).

Through all of the demonic oppression, we knew Jesus was with us. It took more of an overall toll on them rather than me. They had to live and sleep in their house where, almost daily, demonic agitations were occurring. Satan pursued this family, but Jesus won the battle for them.

You should also know that they treated me like I was one of their family. We had meals together, went out to eat, and when Loretta found out I liked oatmeal-raisin cookies, hardly a day went by without a cookie being available. And they knew ice cream was my favorite food, so they made sure I had opportunities to indulge in above average quantities with toppings.

Jesus, the Prince of peace (Isaiah 9:6), is evident as His peace has returned to their faces, and their dogs no longer growl and bark angrily at evil spirits.

Psalm 23

The LORD is my shepherd; I shall not want. He maketh me to lie down in green pastures: He leadeth me beside the still waters. He restoreth my soul: He leadeth me in the paths of righteousness for His Name's sake. Yea, though I walk through the valley of the shadow of death, I will fear no evil: for Thou art with me; Thy rod and Thy staff they comfort me. Thou preparest a table before me in the presence of mine enemies: Thou anointest my head with oil; my cup runneth over. Surely goodness and mercy shall follow me all the days of my life: and I will dwell in the house of the LORD forever.

Speaking the Truth in Love

The title of this chapter is taken from Ephesians 4:15 where we are instructed "to speak the truth in love," so that we will grow up in Christ. No matter how carefully a person presents the truth, there are those who will resent it. Chapter details and facts that will be presented are to benefit all, including the music industry and Hollywood. Sometimes, "words of love filled with truth" are resented, rather than embraced from the heart.

The Bible makes it clear that the LORD *always knows* what is happening everywhere in each person's life. His eyes move to and fro upon the earth. This truth is documented in 1 Kings 8:39, 2 Chronicles 16:9, Proverbs 5:21, and Hebrews 4:13. The saying, "What happens in Las Vegas stays in Las Vegas" is not true. All is fully known by God.

Some people have job descriptions such as chief correspondents or investigative journalists. They do great work at finding facts and exposing them. However, there is no one more accurate than Jesus when it comes to observing and recording facts in the Book of Life (Revelation 20:12-15). He is the Chief Correspondent of the Universe, the true Journalist of facts. He never gives false news, because He is the Lord of Truth (John 14:6).

Today, marriage vows are not taken as seriously as they once were. Divorce is rampant due to adultery, seeking more financial assets, drug addiction problems, advancing careers, physical and verbal abuse, or a combination of these. With solid confidence, I can say that "Hollywood demons" are constantly active and quite successful in preparing couples for divorce. Look at how many stay together for life. And we must not forget that demons are on tour with the numerous singers and music groups. Their drunkenness, drug use, foul language, and "city to city sexual encounters" bear witness.

Because of its music, movies, and the most beautiful people in the world, Hollywood has a tremendous worldwide impact. But much of its impact, according to the Bible, is a sinful impact (Galatians 5:19-21).

Seldom are faith-based family oriented movies produced in comparison to films of violence, sexual encounters, and witchcraft. Jesus and the Bible are mocked. Hollywood, you have the opportunity to influence for good or evil. Why do you select the evil agenda so often?

Also, tabloids are loaded with gossip. People buy them to read about other people's sins and problems when they could use their time more wisely to pray and clean up their own lives.

Often we hear the verbal testimony of actors who have overcome an addiction. They struggle for years and sometimes become ensnared again by the same substance. They might even write a book, which is read by many people. Yet, they seldom seek Jesus for more help and strength, and where is His Name given credit in their books or testimony? You may not like what I say next, but it's true. A person who does not want Christ's help in any problem is telling the One Who took part in creating the Universe (John 1:1-3; Colossians 1:16-17) that His help is of no value to them. Come on people, get a life with reality.

Because I know the Bible, have served Jesus since 1974, and have witnessed His miraculous life-changing power, I am convinced that many of the drug-related deaths among actors and musicians could have been avoided if they had sought the LORD's help. However, in most of Hollywood, the Name of Jesus is considered non-essential or a problem because of what He teaches concerning right and wrong. At times, the wealthy and successful can be hard to reach with truth.

We must not forget that **"demons are vicious soul hunters."** Satan puts up a veil of deception by convincing people their good works will get them into Heaven. So, how many good works does it take? What historical document are you going to use to support your belief? Do you have more love than Jesus has for humanity? Will your love forgive all your sins? Did you come down from Heaven to dwell with humanity? Jesus predicted His resurrection from the dead (John 2:18-22). Can you do this? God's grace of forgiveness comes through faith in Christ's shed blood, death, burial, and His resurrection (1 Corinthians 15:1-4).

Actors, musicians, and celebrities are driven to accomplish greater recognition and make more money for pleasures and investments. But for some, it only brings addictions or hoarding of more and more material possessions. Such people should remember *what* Jesus said: "For what shall it profit a man, if he shall gain the whole world, and lose his soul. Or what shall a man give in exchange for his soul?" (Mark 8:36-37). Demons are working non-stop to train people for suffering in Hell.

I knew before I sat down to type this manuscript that an intense and well-planned spiritual war would be waged against me, supported by demons. It would come in curses and spells from psychics, fortune-tellers, educated witches, and New Age Hollywood celebrities who disagree with me. The reasons why these people will attack me is because of the money they make and the control that is used in witchcraft in various ways. Also, some people don't like Jesus, because His words of love and forgiveness tell them how to live a life dependent on Him for guidance.

People involved with any type of witchcraft want a lifestyle of "My will be done," rather than a lifestyle of "Thy will be done." Such an attitude declares war against Jesus and His followers and harmonizes with the demonic spiritual realm. With whom are you in harmony?

Psychics and Fortune-Tellers: This is how they operate. Some are phonies who guess at what could be happening in your life. Others have demonic help which gives them accurate knowledge of what they reveal. Here is how psychics and fortune-tellers gain information and present hidden things to impress and demonically snare people for money:

1. When you first visit a psychic or fortune-teller, who uses demons for gathering information, a demon will follow you to observe you and listen to conversations to get information about you for the psychic or fortune-teller to reveal during your next visit.

2. Most likely, a demon motivated the person to come in and pay for "a reading" of some kind. That demon will have some "history information" about the customer and will give it to the demon

helping the psychic or fortune-teller, or the demon gives it directly to the mind of the psychic or fortune-teller. When the psychic or fortune-teller presents this private information, this will impress the customer and stimulate a return visit.

3. Upon returning for another reading, the demon working with the psychic or fortune-teller gives any new information seen or heard about that person to the psychic or fortune-teller.

4. Then the psychic or fortune-teller reveals even more private details that have occurred or are occurring in the person's life.

5. This usually convinces the deceived person into believing the psychic or fortune-teller has unique current and future insight on important issues of life. The result can cause an invisible spiritual bond between a demon and the person who sought psychic help.

6. When this bond is established, demon activity will have free access to the residence of the person "paying for information," and the demon(s) involved will influence others in the house.

Without knowing the dark, evil source of psychic and fortune-telling knowledge, misled and desperate people spend millions of dollars every year to get insight from the invisible realm where demons gather information in order to deceive them. Christians need to tell them Jesus and His Bible have all they need (Romans 12:4-8; 1 Corinthians 12:4-11; Ephesians 4:11-12), and the information is forever free.

If you study the family history of psychics and fortune-tellers, it is common to find a family connection to generational witchcraft. Those with any "supernatural knowledge gifts" that manifested from childhood onward usually believe they were born with these paranormal gifts to help people and don't consider them evil. However, until they accept the fact that the Holy Spirit does not distribute any supernatural gifts *until* a person is saved from their sins (becomes born-again, born from above), they will not renounce their occult gift(s). Also, the pride of having a supernatural gift makes it hard to renounce it. People like to control others.

In other cases, people with no history of family occult practices get trained by a psychic or fortune-teller, or they follow occult book guidelines on how to make contact with "a familiar spirit." Then they begin their new occupation of contacting evil spirits for information that controls people, makes money, and spreads fame for themselves.

Psychics, fortune-tellers, witches, and false prophets in Christianity all portray "the sin of presumption," because they try to control the future by speaking their words of future events the way they want them to happen. The sin of presumption is very evil (Deuteronomy 17:12-13; 18:20-22; Psalm 19:13), because it leads people away from the LORD and causes them to serve demonic gods. Holy Spirit words of guidance do not come from a psychic, fortune-teller, or false Biblical prophet.

The psychics, who are used by law enforcement to find out what happened at the scene of a terrible crime, sometimes guess about the ordeal. Or psychics will contact spirits (demons) and tell them to ask other spirits in the spirit realm to gather information about the incident. However, these psychics will deny that any such spiritual input is evil.

Witchcraft and all arts of fortune-telling rake in a lot of money, and anyone making money off of people seeking advice will be upset if the person converts to Christ, because the convert will now get current and future advice *freely* from the Bible and Holy Spirit. When people find out that Christ's power, wisdom, and protection are free and more powerful, they usually submit to Jesus. Christians are called to be imitators of Christ by representing the love, patience, and forgiveness that *only* comes from faith in Jesus.

Decades ago I was at a morning Bible study, and we had a new guest visit us. He was a Christian counselor who used the Bible for counseling, and He helped anyone who came to him for counsel. He related an incident that will shed more light on what power indwells some psychics. He told us that one day at his office, he was moved to pray more than usual before he saw any of his clients. He sensed that there would be a greater need for one of the people he would see.

In one of his open hours, a psychic came in to talk about spiritual problems she was having. He talked to her about Jesus as the best counselor of all. Suddenly, she began shaking uncontrollably. The counselor relaxed, sat back in his recliner, and began to praise Jesus out loud. In a minute, the indwelling demon left her. This demonstrates the fact that some psychics have demons in them that give them "secret information" to pass on to those seeking supernatural direction in life. It also establishes the fact that the Holy Spirit power coming from this Christian counselor was and is *greater* (1 John 4:4) than the evil power that was inside the psychic.

Reiki Healing: This type of energy healing has become quite popular in America. According to 1 Corinthians 12:7-11, the energy power that functions in Reiki healing is not one of the gifts of the Holy Spirit. My book titled *Are Yoga & Reiki Healing Evil?* explains that the healing energy functioning in Reiki healing is not from God's Holy Spirit. The book also reveals some details about Yoga that will interest all readers.

Concerning the demonic war that will target me for years, I will depend on the Lord Jesus, the Holy Spirit, and Christ's holy angels for protection (1 Peter3:22). Friends and churches will also back me with prayer and edification. Definitely, my prayer and praise life will increase. Publishing this book will be costly for me but nothing compared to the sacrificial death my Lord Jesus suffered on the cross to forgive my sins and the sins of all people (John 1:29).

I enjoy listening to music on You Tube. It truly amazes me when I see that some songs have millions of views. This indicates how God has placed in us a desire to enjoy music. The impact of music is beyond belief. But we must use discretion when selecting what comes into ours ears, our mind, and our heart. Music that mocks God and Christ, mocks good morals that respect people, and glorifies Satan and his demons must be rejected. We have seen a history of what drugs, combined with evil lyrics in music, have done from the 1960s till now.

So many of the songs in different genres have words that promote sex. The way singers dance on stage, while performing, makes it look like they are having sex with the air in front of them or with another person. And when some are interviewed, they open up about their sex life. Why can't people keep sex in the bedroom? And why can't they cover more of their bodies? Are they trolling for extra sex attention?

Charlie Rich recorded a beautiful song titled *Behind Closed Doors*. Take the time to listen to it. One of the lines is "No one knows what goes on behind closed doors." That's a wonderful guideline for Hollywood and the rest of the world to follow. Keep your sex life private.

Several years ago, I was in another state working with a pastor to drive demons out of a teenager. Before a demon left, he sarcastically said:

"You Christians are Pawns in a game of chess,
and you are used for suffering by your God."

What this demon said was true. Paul records in Romans 8:36 that "For Thy sake we are killed all the day long; we are accounted as sheep for the slaughter." Everyone in this world is a Pawn for use by Jesus or Satan. The good news for the followers of Christ is that upon death they enter the presence of God (2 Corinthians 5:8). But what about those who are not followers of the Lord Jesus? Those who choose to be "Pawned" by the Devil will join him in a miserable afterlife (Matthew 25:41; Revelation 20:10-15).

In a song, Bob Dylan sang "You gotta serve somebody." These words line up with Biblical teachings. In this world that was created by the LORD, we are given the freedom to choose whom we follow. To make it simple, people serve Jesus, the Lord of love and forgiveness, or the Devil, the lord of darkness and deception.

Hollywood and musicians, are you giving Satan permission to use you as a Pawn of sin and destruction? If you have not asked Jesus to forgive your sins and follow His Biblical teachings, then like I once was, you are following the father of lies (John 8:44-45) who is the "Prince of the power of the air" (Ephesians 2:2).

James 4:14 reveals that our life is brief, like a vapor, here today and gone tomorrow. We have the opportunities to make many good decisions. The Almighty God collects the tears of His people in a bottle (Psalm 56:8) and will one day wipe away every tear of pain, sorrow, and death as we experience eternal life (Revelation 21:4). In the future, do you want Jesus to wipe away every tear of pain, suffering, and death?

Hollywood, you must never forget that you live in an area where one of the most violent spiritual wars is constantly happening. What was once called the City of Angels is now the City of angels and demons. Two supernatural forces fight for this spiritual territory to control the physical lives in the territory below. One force is evil and wants to destroy souls though greed, fame, drugs, and deception, making them think they don't need to have Jesus forgive their sins. The other force is holy and fights to protect people for Jesus, so that souls can hear His Gospel of love and forgiveness and live in Heaven with Him for eternity.

God has set eternity in the hearts of man so that all might know Him (Ecclesiastes 3:11). Luke 19:41 records that Jesus wept over Jerusalem, because He knew some would not believe in Him as their Savior. Is it too hard to picture Jesus standing above the Hollywood sign and saying this?

> Hollywood, Hollywood. As I stood over Jerusalem
> centuries ago, I stand over your sign on a hill calling out
> to you with my love and forgiveness to repent of your sins
> that I might heal your hearts and forgive you for eternity.

Despite what some people think, all who hear the Gospel of God's forgiveness are accountable in this world to receive Christ's love and forgiveness or reject it. Hebrews 9:27 declares that it is appointed for man to die once and judgment comes. There is no second chance after you die. God set it up this way, and it is fair for all people.

We are not born with "a spark of divinity" in us that makes us God's children. We become His children when we are born-again (John 3:3-8) by confessing our sins and committing our life to Jesus. He is in Heaven preparing a place (John 14:1-3) for all who receive Him as the atonement for their sins (1 John 2:2).

The basic definition of "cherish" is beautiful and a heart stimulator. It means "to hold dear, treat with care and affection, and to keep deeply in mind." This is a classic definition of Christ's love for humanity. He came down from His perfect heavenly residence to live with sinful people. Then He showed His love for humanity by shedding His blood, dying on the cross for our sins, and being raised from the dead. By faith in what He did, we can have forgiveness and live in Heaven forever when we pass away.

Make sure you have the real Jesus in your heart (2 Corinthians 13:5). In the world, there are many definitions and beliefs of Who Jesus is, but *only one* is correct. In Matthew 16:15, Jesus asks this question; "Whom do you say that I am?" The Old Testament Scriptures foretold the Redeemer of mankind would be God in human flesh (Isaiah 7:14; 9:6; Micah 5:2).

To verify the accurate history of Jesus' Deity, several New Testament verses also support the Old Testament prophetic declarations that the Son of God would be both God and man (have two natures in one person) when He came to earth (John 1:1-3, 14; 10:30-33; Colossians 1:16-17; 2:9).

The uniqueness of Jesus is celebrated around the world daily as many sing praises to His Name and constantly gather to worship, fellowship, and study the Bible for a more personal relationship with Christ the Lord. Jesus of Nazareth changed the calendars of history (B. C. and A. D.) when He entered our world.

Christmas time reminds the world to celebrate His birth. Easter time reminds the world to celebrate His death on the cross, burial, and physical resurrection (1 Corinthians 15:1-8). He has changed millions of lives for the better. Have you received Jesus (John 1:12) and allowed Him to forgive your sins and change your life for the better?

Please remember that your good works *will not* get you into heaven. God has set a standard of one good work which enables all to enter heaven (John 6:29). We must all accept Christ's good work of forgiveness for our sins on the cross, or we reject God's way (John 14:6). These verses describe God's forgiveness:

> For by grace, are ye saved through faith; that not
> of yourselves: it is the gift of God: Not of works,
> lest any man should boast (Ephesians 2:8-9).

These verses clearly tell us that no person "should boast" of their good works in order to be saved from their sins. Our faith in Jesus, Who is God's grace to us, is a free gift of love and forgiveness which cannot be earned. If we place our faith in Jesus and His redemptive work of forgiveness on the cross, then His shed blood for our sins cleanses us for eternity.

Do you want to leave a legacy to your family and friends of Christ's love and forgiveness, or do you want to leave them a legacy that is void of Christ's love and forgiveness? Do you want them empty of His love or filled with His love? The choice is yours.

Well, Hollywood and talented musicians, out of sincere concern for you I have told you the truth. Jesus changed my life to love people, and that is why I wrote this book. I still hurt when I look back and think of the drug-related deaths and suicides that have destroyed many lives that were blessed with talent. Jesus came to give abundant life, not death (John 10:10). He who has the Son has eternal life (1 John 5:12).

Please consider taking time to listen to a song Faith Hill recorded titled, "There will come a day." It is filled with current and future Biblical truth to help us until we meet Jesus, our Lord of love.

Remember, the inferior supernatural powers of multiple forms of witchcraft might help you get what you want for a while, but in the end it will cost you your soul as Jesus taught in Matthew 16:26. The superior and *holy* supernatural power of Christ's love and forgiveness will reward you and take care of you for eternity.

Will I see you in Heaven?

Contact information:

Danny Frigulti

P. O. Box 169

Visalia, CA 93279

Made in the USA
Las Vegas, NV
23 January 2022